Decision to Prosecute

MIT Studies in American Politics and Public Policy
Jeffrey Pressman and Martha Weinberg, general editors

Decision to Prosecute:
Organization and Public Policy
in the Antitrust Division

Suzanne Weaver

The MIT Press
Cambridge, Massachusetts, and London, England

This book was printed and bound in the United States of America

Second printing, 1978

Library of Congress Cataloging in Publication Data

Weaver, Suzanne.
  Decision to prosecute.

  (MIT studies in American politics and public policy ; 2)
  Includes bibliographical references and index.
  1. United States. Dept. of Justice. Antitrust Division. 2. Antitrust
law—United States. I. Title. II. Series.
KF1653.W4   343'.73'072   77–6449
ISBN 0–262–23085–2

Contents

Editors' Foreword

Social scientists have increasingly directed their attention toward defining and understanding the field of public policy. Until recently public policy was considered to be a product of the actions of public institutions and as such was treated as the end point in analysis of the governmental process. But in recent years it has become clear that the public policy-making process is infinitely more complex than much of the literature of social science would imply. Government institutions do not act in isolation from each other, nor is their behavior independent of the substance of the policies with which they deal. Furthermore, arenas of public policy do not remain static; they respond to changes in their political, organizational, and technical environments. As a result, the process of making public policy can best be understood as one that involves a complicated interaction between government institutions, actors, and the particular characteristics of substantive policy areas.

The MIT Press series, *American Politics and Public Policy,* is made up of books that combine concerns for the substance of public policies with insights into the working of American political institutions. The series aims at broadening and enriching the literature on specific institutions and policy areas. But rather than focusing on either institutions or policies in isolation, the series features those studies that help describe and explain the environment in which policies are set. It includes books that examine policies at all stages of their development—formulation, execution, and implementation. In addition, the series features studies of public actors —executives, legislatures, courts, bureaucracies, professionals, and the media—that emphasize the political and organizational constraints under which they operate. Finally, the series includes books that treat public policy making as a process and help explain how policy unfolds over time.

Suzanne Weaver's book on the Antitrust Division of the Department of Justice clearly conveys a sense of the agency's history, personality, and style, and convincingly shows how these characteristics affect Justice Department policy making. Weaver devotes special attention to the important question of what accounts for innovation and change in a "technical" organization and provides a thoughtful and thorough analysis of the effect of professional norms on policy outcomes. In addition, Weaver gives detailed attention to the development of government regulation of business and sets Antitrust's philosophy and standards in a broad historical and philosophical context. In doing so, she provides not only a full and rich study of one important agency but also deals with the implications of that agency's behavior for other institutions of government and for the policy-making process.

Professor Weaver teaches at Yale University.

Jeffrey Pressman
Martha Weinberg

Decision to Prosecute

1
Introduction

Since the late 1960s, public discussion has entered one of its periods of special preoccupation with the role of wealth and big business in American life. A small army of scholars, journalists, social
critics, and legislators has turned its energies to the task of telling
us that our tax laws make the rich richer and the poor poorer, that
business not only deceives and robs us but endangers our lives,
and that economic power is unacceptably concentrated. As in the
1880s and the 1930s, the opinion has grown that a good part of the
nation's social and economic ills stems from power exercised badly (or exercised at all) by corporations and those who run them—
and that their motives and behavior are opposed to the interests of
the public as a whole.

Along with this opinion has come a growing feeling that the
means we have relied on to bring business into harmony with the
public interest have proved inadequate. The failures have been
alleged in areas from taxation policy and campaign financing to
environmental policy and congressional organization, and over
the past decade the allegations have spurred a substantial body of
reform. But one of the chief targets of criticism has been the group
of federal agencies charged directly with the regulation and control of business behavior.

The verdict has become nearly unanimous that our regulatory
system works badly. Some critics contend that the agencies fail
because they have fallen victim to the dark side of American plur-
alism, to co-optation or "clientalism." The regulatory agencies,
these critics argue, were established to promote a public interest
that could not be served by the free play of private interests in the
marketplace. But as general public attention to their activities
waned while the regulated interests maintained a well-financed
vigilance, the agencies eventually abandoned their proper goals
and began to cater to the private interests they were supposed to
restrain.[1]

Other critics point to further reasons for regulatory failure. It is
claimed, for instance, that outside political forces—Congress, the
White House, and the parties—often intervene in regulatory decisions to ensure that they do not threaten the powerful; or that
politicians conspire tacitly, through the budget and appointment
processes, to keep the agencies underfunded and their executives

inoffensive.[2] Still other critics emphasize that the agencies suffer from an abysmal lack of clarity about their goals and standards and that this confusion of itself makes it impossible for them to fulfill their intended purposes.[3] Finally, there are those, still more radical in their explanations, who argue that regulation has failed not because the agencies have been diverted from serving the public interest but because they were never intended to serve the public interest in the first place. Many agencies, these critics hold, were created as mere symbolic gratifications to the public, and for some the conscious purpose was actually to provide benefits and protection to the business interests that were put under agency jurisdiction. It therefore requires no recourse to theories of co-optation or corruption, these last critics say, to see why they have not served the nation as a whole.[4]

Such criticisms, while they have reached a notably high level in recent years, are hardly unprecedented in American public discourse. And in a slightly earlier time they would have been thought to carry with them fairly predictable policy implications. We would have been told, and were told, that we needed measures to make personal corruption more difficult among regulatory employees, that we needed a tightening of the standards that regulatory agencies applied, and that we needed a president and Congress with the political will to appoint men who were better, more honest, more devoted to the public interest and disdainful of the blandishments that the regulated could offer.

But, increasingly, we are not being told such things; the older remedies are coming to be thought insufficient. For whatever reason—because the critics' antagonism to American business is deeper than it has ever been or because events have given many among them a deeper mistrust of executive discretion altogether—regulatory solutions that leave broad formal discretionary power in the hands of administrative agencies are coming to be looked on as the precursors, almost necessarily, of further abuse. The "interest group liberalism" that has been described in these regulatory agencies, and that Theodore Lowi has described more broadly for various sectors of our government, seems to such critics inherently corrupt.[5]

What we need in the regulatory area, it is increasingly said, is what we need in so many other areas of American public policy: a government of laws and not of men. Sometimes the proposals that flow from this perspective are straightforward, as with the growing sentiment for out-and-out deregulation of some regulated industries.[6] Other such proposals would shift control of regulatory policy to different bodies, as with the wave of new environmental and health and safety regulations in which Congress has made the bounds of agency discretion narrower than ever before. Sometimes they recommend that the courts take a more active role in limiting regulatory agency discretion.[7] Sometimes they concern themselves with constricting the discretionary influence that politicians can exercise over the legal jobs that government does, as with our current enthusiasm for the device of the independent prosecutor. We seem to have moved beyond the simple notion that public power should take precedence over private economic power: Now the distinctions have been refined. Public power should take precedence over private power; but because public power exercised with administrative discretion often does not properly do so, we should prefer those forms of regulation that give political executives the least of that discretion. What discretion exists should go to Congress and the courts; government executives should be forced to take direction from and be closely accountable to these other bodies.

We assume, when we make such recommendations, that we do so out of some empirical knowledge about the consequences of using the older, regulatory commission form to supervise the affairs of business. But, as it happens, we also have at least some idea of what the results of more reliance on alternative forms of regulation might be. The Antitrust Division of the Department of Justice has since the beginning of the twentieth century been dealing with business in ways very different from those of the regulatory commissions, and in ways that the commissions' newer critics might be expected to find more acceptable.

The job of the Antitrust Division is to enforce various statutes governing the conduct of American business organizations and the structure of the sectors of American economy. Chief among these statutes are the Sherman Act[8] and the Clayton Act.[9] The Sherman Act prohibits firms and individuals from monopolizing any line of commerce, attempting to monopolize it, conspiring to monopolize it, or combining or conspiring with others to restrain trade in any line of commerce. The Clayton Act prohibits both a number of specific monopolistic or restrictive practices and acquisition of one firm by another when the effect of the acquisition may be to lessen competition substantially or tend to create a monopoly in any line of commerce. The Antitrust Division is charged with identifying violators of these laws and prosecuting them in federal courts to secure their punishment or relief from the harm done by their violations.

To do its job, the division had a fiscal year 1977 budget of approximately twenty-five million dollars and employed 463 professional staff members, including 40 economists and 423 lawyers. Of the lawyers, about two-thirds usually operate from the division's main office in Washington, while the rest are distributed among field offices in other cities. The staff lawyers are, for purposes of salary and tenure, civil servants. The main responsibility of most of them is to investigate possible violations of the antitrust laws, to recommend whether prosecution should be instituted, and to try the cases that result if they are not otherwise settled. The attorneys are supervised in these tasks by their "career" superiors—section chiefs and a director of operations—and by their assistant attorney general, the politically appointed head of the division. The AAG, in turn, is formally responsible to the head of the Department of Justice, the attorney general; until very recently, the attorney general routinely had the final formal word on whether to bring the cases that the division proposed.[10]

If a case is approved for prosecution, the division may proceed in one of two ways. Either the case may be taken to trial in the courts, or—if the case is not a criminal one—it may be settled with a consent decree, an agreement between the government and the defendant. This agreement is submitted to the court without a trial and if the court approves, it acquires the same binding force as a court order that emerges after a full-scale trial. Since 1940, the division has brought an average of forty cases a year, the majority of which have been settled through the consent decree procedure.[11]

It might be argued that the Antitrust Division is a poor organization to compare with other regulatory agencies: When we speak of regulation and regulatory agencies, we usually are referring to a task and a set of government organizations that seem to differ substantially from those in the antitrust arena. Much regulation supersedes market competition rather than seeking to enforce it; most regulatory agencies have a complex and many-sided mandate rather than a relatively unified one; and much of the regulatory agencies' activity goes on outside the rules and relationships directly imposed by the federal courts. Each of these distinctions does have important organizational and political consequences. But none of them overrides the basic similarities between the division and other government organizations that seek to control business conduct.

For one thing, the limited resources of the division, when compared to the size of the American economy, require that many of the organization's decisions will be decisions not to prosecute, decisions that are unlikely to emerge into the courtroom or its adversary process. Even more important, the relatively simple mandate of the division is still complex and ambiguous enough to leave prosecutors considerable room for other kinds of discretionary interpretation as well. It is left to the judicial process—to the courts, of course, but also to prosecutors and plaintiffs, who set the agenda for the courts—to decide what specific practices and conditions are to be considered in violation of the law. The substantive content of the laws cannot by itself determine whether the Antitrust Division will act strictly as an advocate in these decisions or will assume a quasi-judicial role, whether the enforcement relationship between government and business will be a purely adversary one or will include elements of bargaining and cooperation, whether the enforcers will try to maximize the predictability of their actions or seek ongoing changes in the laws' scope. In the same way, one cannot know in advance but must instead ask whether antitrust enforcement has been guided by external economic considerations in deciding on its program—considerations of the national distribution of income, the balance of payments, the state of the stock market, the level of unemployment, product development, or mobility of labor and capital. Moreover, the language of these laws left the prosecutors considerable discretion in interpreting their broader meaning. The terms of the Sherman and

Clayton acts—terms such as "restraint of trade," "monopolization," "line of commerce," "lessening of competition"—are not
self-explanatory. What they mean depends significantly on one's
concept of the larger purpose of the antitrust laws, and this purpose has been—and still is—the subject of vigorous debate.

Finally, the division resembles its more conventional regulatory
counterparts in another crucial respect. The antitrust laws were
passed and began to be enforced in a period of intense popular
interest in the subject of American business structure and practices. After this initial interest subsided, enforcement continued in
an atmosphere of relative obscurity that has been only sporadically
interrupted. And while public attention flagged, the businessmen
subject to the laws kept an attentive interest in their enforcement.
This is the same combination of circumstances that attended the
birth and growth of many other regulatory agencies and that gave
rise to many of the major theories about their malaise.

What chiefly distinguishes the Antitrust Division from other regulatory agencies established from the end of the last century until
the latter part of this one is that, with antitrust, resolving these ambiguities was a task given as a routine matter to the courts and,
therefore, to the advocates who make their cases to the courts.
Enough features of our antitrust policy are sui generis so that one is
not tempted into overly schematic assertions about the effect of
one or another organizational feature on the present state of enforcement. But by looking at the way the Antitrust Division uses
the discretion available to it, one can learn something about the
consequences of this court-oriented form of policy making.

The present study chose to look at this discretion by asking one
question: "Why does the division choose to bring any particular
case?" By asking this question, one slights several of the organization's activities that do not involve decisions about whether to
prosecute: the process of appeal to higher courts, the supervision
of court orders already handed down, division participation in certain kinds of legislative and interagency affairs, and the process by
which the organization reaches particular terms of settlement with
businesses in the process of formulating consent decrees. The focus on prosecution, however, seems justified. Not only does the
organization devote the vast majority of its staff time to investiga-

tion and prosecution of cases but the organization's sense of itself as an essentially prosecutorial unit pervasively affects the way it performs its other functions.

To find out how the division brings its cases, I interviewed approximately one hundred division staff members, as well as members of the division's front office, division alumni, other members of the private antitrust bar, Office of Management and Budget officials, congressional staff members, and journalists who have long observed the organization. The staff interviews included questions about personal background and careers, views of the antitrust task, and relations with other members of the division and outsiders; but the bulk of these interviews consisted of questions about individual cases the staff member had participated in—origins, reasons for various decisions made in the course of investigation, recommendations, reasons for those recommendations, the fate of these recommendations at higher levels in the organization, and the reasons given for these higher-level decisions. The interviews most frequently lasted from one hour and forty-five minutes to two hours, and many interviews lasted considerably longer than that. The original interviews were conducted in 1971; several more staff interviews were conducted in 1974, and conversations and published material to date have been used to ensure that this picture remains essentially accurate.

Any one staff member tends to handle relatively few separate investigations and thus tends to remember those matters he has been involved with; this helped produce detailed information about several hundred investigations, from origin to disposition, and a fairly firm basis on which to generalize about the division. The research was limited by two restrictions the division imposed: I was not supposed to discuss any investigation by name with the staff, and I was not formally permitted to see written internal communications. The first restriction did little harm: I was rarely centrally interested in the names of particular cases, the names were often easy enough to guess, and the restriction proved very difficult for attorneys to abide by in practice. The second restriction was a serious disadvantage. Although the written material that did come my way gave me no cause to believe that the interviews seriously distorted the true picture of how these decisions were made, the research would of course have benefited from more systematic access to the record.

The picture that emerged from these interviews and from the documentary research that supplemented them was of an organization that does reflect, though sometimes in ironic ways, the larger tensions and uncertainties that the country has experienced in coming to its opinions about antitrust policy. In chapter 2, I used the available historical research to make some observations about the nature of the public policy that the Antitrust Division came to be responsible for. One impression that emerges quite powerfully from a look at this history is that despite our natural wish to find as coherent an intention as possible in the minds of our antitrust founders and their attentive public, their words simply cannot satisfy us on this score. The language that is familiar to us as students of economics and economic policy is accompanied by the language of Jeffersonian politics, and the potential contradictions between the two simply did not occupy the original public discussion of antitrust. Our antitrust policy today comes under cogent criticism for its lack of policy coherence,[12] and it is in the most natural of American traditions that we should want to find a major source of this failing in the corruption visited upon our policy intentions by our administrative arrangements. But before one exaggerates the extent of such corruption, one might do well to ask how much of what we now have is to be found in the policy-formation process itself. We already have evidence from other areas of domestic policy that administration comes to reflect legislative intention—or lack thereof—to an extent we have not enough recognized;[13] the field of antitrust provides us with yet more evidence on the question.

One special consequence of the intentions of our antitrust founders is that antitrust policy came to be enforced through the mechanism of prosecutors and courts, and chapter 3 begins to examine that consequence. We have learned that a crucial aid in explaining how an organization makes its decisions is to know why its members joined it and why they stay there. In the Antitrust Division, it emerges, a significant number of the operatives, the staff attorneys, have joined or remain because they want to bring antitrust cases and win them. Their goals and opinions are overwhelmingly those that one associates with legal advocates and prosecutors, and their opinions on various questions that are important in shaping antitrust enforcement are largely determined by the imperatives of prosecution. As in the case of most organizations with complex mandates, the Antitrust staff has in effect narrowed theirs; but the choices that have been made have not been unrelated to the nature of the legislation guiding the organization.

Chapter 4 turns from the general opinions of the Antitrust staff to the question of what patterns can be seen in their decisions about individual cases—and finds that the case decisions are of a piece with the more general views. These are people who do want vigorous enforcement of the antitrust laws—which means that they want to bring and win as many cases as possible. The chief constraint on them, they feel, is that in fact the environment does not easily produce for them a large number of case possibilities from which to choose. So most of their time is spent investigating information that turns out to present no reasonable possibility of being an opportunity for prosecution. When an opportunity does emerge, the staff will be energetic in seeking to develop it into an actual case, and it will be quite unabashedly partisan in its use of arguments.

The next three chapters look at what one might expect to be sources of challenge to this staff ethos, observe that the challenge does not emerge, and try to explain why. Chapters 5 and 6 deal with the executive levels of the organization—which have a substantial effect on the organization's product through their review of cases and through their proposals for new antitrust initiatives but which consistently exercise this influence in behalf of principles that are not very different from those of the staff attorneys themselves. In part this consistency comes from a simple coincidence of views; but where executives have actually tried to exercise authority in behalf of goals different from those of the staff, they have found that staff resistance and the outside opinion that supports it can make the exercise futile in the long run. And chapter 7 argues that these same opinions provide even more protection for the division from politicians and businessmen on the outside who might want to interfere in its activities. This insulation is perhaps surprising, in light of what we tend to believe about external influence in regulatory matters, but it is real nevertheless. The place of the division in the court process and the kind of professionalism that place induces may narrow the way in which the organization exercises its mandate, but they also protect it from some kinds of pressures that we have come to view as illegitimate. Chapter 8, finally, talks about the balance that the division has struck among the various considerations that might be expected to influence our regulatory agencies and about how this balance can be compared with some available alternatives.

2
Organization and Intention

A persistent theme in the treatment that American public discourse has given to government-business relations has been the theme of corruption—corruption not only as venality but as a distortion of the proper relationship between public authority and private power. The theme is lent a special resonance by at least two of our long-standing concerns. The first, of course, is our historic and pervasive mistrust of the motives and power of big business, even during those times when we have been most publicly enthusiastic about the free-market principle. But just as important and at least as long-standing, we have until recently tended to govern business in large part through the discretionary power of bureaucracies—a power that has carried a stigma even when we have expected the most from central government. Bureaucracy, so the argument goes, is a form of power specially prone to pervert the public purposes entrusted to it: If business is the institution among us specially eager to corrupt, bureaucracy is an institution specially ready to be corrupted.

The field of antitrust, like other areas of government-business relations, has been much influenced by the notion that high legislated public purposes are in constant danger of being distorted and turned to low ends. With antitrust, in particular, we tend to take the law as something relatively clear and certainly natural to us. It seems only natural that a regime whose speech gives such frequent and prominent praise to the virtues of competition should embody this opinion in its public law. But in fact the antitrust laws did not spring quickly or easily from a consensual commitment to free enterprise or the competitive system. For one thing, public animus against economic power and restrictive business practices has by no means been uniformly intense throughout our history. For another, even those most committed to the idea of the free market have not been united in a demand for public action against imperfections in that market or in their ideas of what form public action should take. Antitrust legislation was not a fully "natural" growth, even in America; the way it emerged has had important consequences for the organization of antitrust enforcement today.

Historians point to the Grange—the Patrons of Animal Husbandry—as the source of the first politically significant complaints against post–Civil War business structure and practices.[1] The Grange, a farm association organized in the 1870s, complained about the high prices that farmers were forced to pay to the railroads that transported their products and about the additional burdens imposed by other suppliers, such as grain elevator operators, farm machinery manufacturers, and banks. Further, the Grange complained of other practices on the part of these suppliers that involved treating equals unequally: The Grange contended, for instance, that the railroads were discriminatory in the rebates they granted various customers.

These grievances gave rise to Grange demands for two kinds of public action. The first demand was for government regulation of railroad rates and practices. The Grange accepted the railroad industry as one in which ownership would always be highly concentrated and in which the requirements of capital investment and scale efficiences would always necessitate the existence of at least some local monopolies. The Grange's arguments assumed, in other words, that the prevailing structure of ownership and service in the railroad industry would continue unchanged. So it was never claimed that the proper remedy was to restore competitive conditions in the industry and to subject the railroads to the rigors of the market. Instead, the Grange solution was to place the industry under a system of public controls that would simply forbid objectionable practices. Indeed, the very fact of industry concentration was taken to mean that such control would be particularly easy and effective.

But the Grange's second demand for government action made somewhat different assumptions. This second demand was broader and less specific than the first: It was a demand for the extirpation of monopoly in most of the lines of commerce on which Grange spokesmen declared farmers to be dependent. For most of these lines of commerce, government regulation—even regulation that would outlaw objectionable prices and practices —was not assumed to be necessary. Instead, the proper remedy for their ills was to restore competitive industry structures. For most industries, in other words, the Grange demands did not concede that concentrated ownership was inevitable or irremediable. The cure for their abuses lay not in the imposition of public, non-market standards upon business but in a public guarantee that a competitive marketplace would be allowed to operate according to its own rules and imperatives.

This Grange attitude toward monopoly revealed assumptions about the connection between economic structure and economic performance that were broadly consistent with the understanding provided by the dominant classical economics of the day. An absence of monopoly would curb excessive prices because free competition contained its own guards against such excesses; an absence of monopoly would mitigate the problem of unfair concessions because it would create competitors willing to cater on more favorable terms to those discriminated against by the unfair concessions.

But it would be misleading to understand the Grange program as a body of well-developed economic theory. For one thing, many traditional economists of the time—those with whom the Grange shared its concern that competitive conditions prevail—tended to argue that government action was not necessary and was perhaps a barrier to the achievement of this goal. Such economists argued that in the long run—and in a market that was free from interference except for that of the monopolists in question—monopolies would either cause their own destruction by setting prices high enough so that the profits would attract competition or, if the monopolies chose to keep prices and profits low enough to discourage potential competitors, would do little ultimate harm to consumers. The Grange, by contrast, displayed no such thoroughgoing faith in the free market's ultimate beneficence or at least showed little interest in the "long run." The Grange organization's pronouncements placed public action on the subject of business paramount; they did not find it necessary to rebut possible objections from theoretical economists.

More important, Grange statements failed to clarify exactly what was meant by the use of the word "monopoly." One can find no clue to that meaning in the "Granger laws" passed by several western and midwestern states; those laws dealt only with the regulation of railroad rates and practices and made no attempt to deal with questions of ownership and control.[2] Neither do public pronouncements by farmers' organizations, conventions, and

Grange-backed third-party planks and candidates identify more precisely the nature of the complaint—hardly a surprising failing, since such statements are intended to exhort and rouse rather than to make distinctions. On the one hand, speakers often referred to monopoly in its structural sense, as exclusive possession of the trade in some commodity or service, or, by extension, possession that was too tightly held to permit truly competitive conditions:[3]

Monopoly names the price of what the agricultural masses have to sell, and charges them what it pleases for what they are compelled to buy. . . . Individual effort is fruitless. The relentless, remorseless, and unyielding grasp of monopoly is upon every avenue of trade and commerce. . . . Trust is only another name for monopoly.

In contrast, attention was also called to specific offensive business practices the remedy for which was not necessarily a structural one. A recurrent objection to the monopolies of the day was that they were extending their influence beyond the economic sphere to the political one, that they were "wielding a greater power in the government than the people." Other statements called attention to offensive practices that could exist in the absence of monopoly: In 1874, the demand of the Illinois Anti-Monopoly Party was for legislation that would "secure the industrial and producing interests of the country against all forms of corporate monopoly and extortion."[4] Another branch of the antimonopoly movement, the Illinois State Farmers' Association, broadened its indictment to proclaim that "every combination to increase the price above what is just and legitimate is a conspiracy against the rights of the people, and a robbery which we loudly protest against."[5]

These statements are by no means inconsistent, but they do suggest that the Grange was simultaneously protesting all economic concentration, extreme economic concentration, and practices that could accompany economic concentration or exist without it. The movement cared less for making fine distinctions among these phenomena than for taking some kind of public action toward the businesses that produced them; the particular form of remedy that the Grange had in mind was therefore less than perfectly clear.

The second body of antitrust opinion that historians cite as significant is the broader attack on the "trusts" that succeeded the protests of the waning Granger and rural antimonopoly movement in the 1880s. This broader public animus against the trusts arose not only among small businessmen competing with bigger ones but also among large numbers of Americans who dealt with the trusts mainly as citizens and consumers, not as members of any special producer interest. The chief organs of this animus were the daily press and semipopular books and periodical magazines.

One problem that tends to confuse any discussion of the nature of the public mandate behind the Sherman Act is that much of the popular literature one usually associates with the attack on the trusts—the muckraking literature, for instance, or Henry Demarest Lloyd's *Wealth Against Commonwealth,* or the reports of the three Chicago Conferences on Trusts—did not appear until after the passage of the act in 1890. This is not to say, of course, that such writings and the opinions they expressed had no effect on the history of antitrust law and its enforcement; the years in which they appeared saw the bringing of some spectacular antitrust cases, the beginning of special congressional appropriations for antitrust enforcement, and, finally, the passage of the Clayton Act in 1914. But these later writings are problematic as guides to the reasons for which the Sherman Act itself was passed; one can avoid this problem by following Hans Thorelli's distinction and focusing on expressions of antitrust opinion in the general literature only up to 1890.

These writings are ambiguous in their antitrust prescriptions in almost the same way that the agrarian antimonopoly movement was ambiguous. The popular press, as Thorelli has noted, was full of criticism of the "trusts"—a word used to refer to a wide variety of forms of business combination.[6] In 1888, Charles Francis Adams proposed what he called an "innocent" plan for increasing coordination among railroads only to see that as soon as it was announced, it was "characterized in the papers as a vast 'trust'—in these days everything is a 'trust'—and denounced as a conspiracy."[7] Whether or not Adams's plan was truly "innocent," it is difficult to tell whether what was under attack was mainly concentration of ownership, or conspiracy among independent producers, or objectionable practices by businessmen acting independently.

It is more difficult to distinguish among these possible complaints because the method of attack in the press seems most often to have been to choose a particular market whose producers could be accused of all these sins at once and to describe it in great and concrete detail. The *New York Times,* for instance, devoted a good deal of attention to the trust question between the years 1887 and 1890, the great bulk of it critical. But if one accepts Thorelli's catalog of *Times* coverage as accurate, one must conclude that almost all that coverage proceeded by exposing specific evils in the largest and best-known trusts. Even the *Times* editorials, where one might expect to find more general reflections on the trust problem, tended to criticize specific behavior by the sugar trust, the linseed oil trust, the cotton oil trust, the lead trust; the editorials commented on "trusts" in general only rarely, and they did not suggest remedies that might have revealed which element of the problem they took to be most important.[8] Press attention to the issue was vocal and sustained, but no more than the Granger movement was it at pains to distinguish among the various purposes for which government might wish to intervene in the operations of the trusts.[9]

One might expect a somewhat more systematic view of the problem from the popular book-length treatments of the subjects of monopoly, trusts, and maldistribution of resources in general. But Henry George's *Progress and Poverty* took land monopoly to be the sole source of the then-current evil practices and maldistributions.[10] Edward Bellamy's *Looking Backward* presented private monopoly as in fact preferable to the working of the free market.[11] And Henry Demarest Lloyd's early articles concerned themselves mainly with exposing specific abuses.[12] These treatments did not supply what the press had failed to provide.

Ironically, those bodies of opinion that produced the clearest and most comprehensive views of the monopoly problem had by far the least effect on the genesis of the Sherman Act. The legislators paid little explicit attention to the writings of serious economic thinkers, and when the congressmen did happen to use arguments provided by these writers, they did so in ways the authors would hardly have approved of.

The most widely read books on economics during the period were probably those of Adam Smith and John Stuart Mill, neither of whom gave much support to the idea of governmental interventions in the working of the free market.[13] And the view among academic economists was more radically laissez-faire than the mention of Smith and Mill would indicate. For while one may easily point to qualifications that these two authors placed on their approval of the unimpeded market, fewer such qualifications appeared in the work of the dominant American writers. Arthur L. Perry, for instance, argued that almost all restraints on trade would in the long run be destroyed by the forces of competition; those restraints that persisted in the long run, he argued, could do so only by virtue of artificial privileges granted by government, and the solution to these long-term imperfections obviously lay not in additional government intervention but in repealing those interventionist policies that supported the imperfections. Other influential economic thinkers of the day, such as Herbert Spencer and William Graham Sumner, also opposed public intervention on the trust question.[14]

When one goes on to consider the less orthodox economists of the period, it should be borne in mind that it was not their view but the classicist one that was dominant. Certainly in the debates on the Sherman Act there was no reference to any views but those of the more orthodox economists, turned though those views were to slightly heretical purposes.

Still, the opinion dominant among economists was not without opposition among economic thinkers during the 1880s, and such opposition centered around some members of the American Economic Association, founded in 1885. William Letwin claims that the AEA was the "official spokesman" of "the general opinion of American economists"[15] at the time, though the association was not a strictly professional one and counted among its members well-known ministers associated with the Social Gospel movement.[16] In any event, the AEA did include the most prominent younger economists who rejected the notion of the inviolability of the market and its workings.[17]

These younger economists—Simon Patten is perhaps the best known—agreed with the orthodox opinion in favoring economic concentration to the extent that it represented an increase in efficiency through economies of scale. They disagreed with some, though not all, of the classicists in accepting the then-growing degree of economic concentration in America as a "natural" phenomenon, not the mere result of artificial privileges conferred by government. Indeed, these younger economists pointed specifically to the large number of industries that could or did benefit from these efficiencies of scale. These heterodox economists devoted a significant amount of their writing to praise of this new, technology-born efficiency.[18]

This enthusiasm for efficiencies of scale was associated with another major feature of this heterodox economic thought: its distaste for laissez-faire economics and for unregulated competition in general. A classical economist might argue that while efficiencies of scale were all to the good, concentration beyond this point of efficiency was bad because it unnecessarily robbed the economy of the benefits of competition, and government intervention was not the way to deal with either phenomenon. A heterodox response would have emphasized how much of the increasing concentration in America was in fact justified by increased efficiency and added that, in any event, one need not worry overmuch about the bad effects of concentration because one need not allow businessmen with market power to make business decisions independently. One could instead regulate those decisions through public agencies, thus preserving the benefits of size while ensuring that the public interest rather than private self-interest would dictate the rules of business behavior.

This heterodox position, then, did lend support to the idea of major government intervention in the marketplace, but it was not to be intervention primarily in behalf of competition pure and simple. The position came to grips with the phenomenon of increasing concentration and the likelihood that this concentration would not decline through the natural erosive forces of an unregulated market, but this opinion also regarded the increasing concentration as potentially beneficial and in any case inevitable. "If it is for the interest of men to combine," one of these economists wrote, "no law can make them compete."[19] Economic concentration would have to be publicly regulated, but not for the primary purpose of preventing anticompetitive practices; indeed, the public regulation envisioned was one that in important respects denied the primacy of competitive values.

An examination of economists' views is thus of little help in discovering the rationale for a government antitrust policy; and it is not surprising that one can find very little evidence of the direct influence of professional economists in the legislative history of the Sherman Act of 1890. For it was not expert opinion but a much less clearly defined popular opinion that inspired Congress to act on the trust question. And because this salient body of opinion was so diffuse and gave the legislators so little guidance as to the form of the public action that should be taken, it is important to describe how the legislators themselves interpreted the problem.

Senator John Sherman initiated the passage of the Sherman Act when, on July 10, 1888, he introduced a resolution calling for consideration by the Senate Finance Committee of a bill[20]

to set aside, control, restrain, or prohibit all arrangements, contracts, agreements, trusts, or combinations . . . which tend to prevent free and full competition in the production, manufacture, or sale of articles of domestic growth or production, or of the sale of articles imported into the United States or which, against public policy, are designed or tend to foster monopoly or artificially advance the cost to the consumer of necessary articles of human life, with . . . provisions . . . as will tend to preserve freedom of trade and production, the natural competition of increasing production, and the lowering of prices by such competition. . . .

The committee to which the resolution was directed for consideration was Sherman's own, and on August 14, 1888, he introduced his own antitrust bill into the committee, a bill that used words almost identical to those of the resolution in describing the category of business arrangements Sherman wished to have declared unlawful and liable to forfeiture of corporate franchises.

The bill that was eventually enacted in 1890 was by no means the same as Sherman's original version. In the two years between introduction and passage, it had been extensively amended and had its jurisdiction changed to that of the Judiciary Committee. The bill that emerged from the Judiciary Committee on April 2, 1890, was essentially the same as the act in its final form; and when one compares the text of the final Sherman Act with Sherman's original resolution, one can see that considerable substitution and changes had been made in the interim.

Nevertheless, Sherman's original resolution embodied the same

philosophy that animated the ultimate Sherman Act. Sherman himself, though he was upset that the bill had been taken away from
his committee, defended the Judiciary Committee's version in the
final debates, saying that it was "the best under all circumstances
that the Senate is prepared to give in this direction."[21] Sherman
also said that he took the final bill's objective to be the same as his
own original aims.[22]

Many of the changes made in the bill from introduction to passage came about because of disagreement over Congress's constitutional power in the area of commerce and further disputes over
enforcement procedures and penalties; these two areas were also
the sources of the chief objections that several congressmen made
to various versions of the bill during the course of the two-year
debate on its passage.[23] With one or two exceptions, the legislators did not publicly object to the basic premise that government
must take action of some kind on the problem of the trusts, to the
Sherman bill's definition of the problem, or to the general nature
of the remedies proposed.[24] So one is fairly safe in looking to the
debates, and to Sherman's speeches in particular, as a critical
source of information about the basic congressional idea of the
abuses to be remedied and the proper remedy for them.

Sherman defended himself in several long speeches against
charges by his colleagues that the bill was either unconstitutional
or without much hope of having any great effect. And the way he
defended himself was to elaborate on the theme that *some* public
action had to be taken against the trusts. "The popular mind," he
said,[25]

is agitated with problems that may disturb the social order, and
among them all none is more threatening than the inequality of
condition, of wealth and opportunity that has grown within a single generation out of the concentration of vast combinations of
capital to control production and trade and to break down competition. These combinations already defy or control powerful transportation corporations and reach state authorities. They reach out
their Briarean arms to every part of our country. They are imported
from abroad. Congress alone can deal with them, and if we are
unwilling or unable there will soon be a trust for every production
and a master to fix the price of every necessity of life.

At another point, Sherman elaborated on what he took to be the
nature of the trust problem:[26]

They had monopolies and mortmains of old, but never before such giants as in our day. You must heed their [the voters] appeal or be ready for the socialist, the communist, and the nihilist. Society is now disturbed by forces never felt before. . . .

The sole purpose of such a combination as that covered by the bill is to make competition impossible. It can control the market, raise or lower prices, as will best promote its selfish interests, reduce prices in a particular locality and break down competition and advance prices at will where competition does not exist. . . . The law of selfishness, uncontrolled by competition, compels it to disregard the interest of the consumer. It dictates terms to transportation companies, it commands the price of labor without fear of strikes, for in its field it allows no competitors. . . . It is this kind of combination we have to deal with now.

If we will not endure a king as a political power we should not endure a king over the production, transportation, and sale of any of the necessaries of life. If we would not submit to an emperor we should not submit to an autocrat of trade, with power to prevent competition and to fix the price of any commodity.

Sir, the object aimed at by this bill is to secure competition of the productions of different states which necessarily enter into interstate and foreign commerce.

These words, which have often been quoted, exhibit ambiguities similar to those of popular opinion on the trust question. It is not surprising, therefore, that these passages have given rise to divergent views of Sherman's intentions. On the one hand, Sherman spoke in these debates of "monopolies," of "combinations," of "concentration," and of arrangements whose purpose was "to break down competition." Though these terms are not fully interchangeable, their meaning seems clear: It seems as if Sherman was speaking, much as a modern economist would, of market power and its inherent tendency to raise prices to the consumer. By this interpretation, what Sherman had in mind for his bill was simply to prohibit artificial price increases and restrictions of output to the detriment of the economic welfare of consumers. As Robert Bork has persuasively argued, there is nothing in Sherman's speeches that explicitly contradicts such an interpretation of Sherman's intentions.[27]

Yet there remains the troubling problem of the words Sherman used in defense of his position, words that suggest that for him the trusts were a political problem that was more than simply a consequence of their economic inefficiencies.[28] Sherman embellished his description of the problem the country faced, and he embellished it in two ways. First, he called special and repeated attention to the absolute size of the objectionable combinations, in addition to their market power. Second, he called attention to their intent. Sherman spoke of "vast" combinations, combinations whose "purpose" was to break down competition, actors of whom it could be said that their "sole object" was to make competition impossible, "giants" whose status was somehow different from that of monopolies that had existed in previous times, agents motivated not be mere self-interest but by "selfishness," companies that could not only advance prices artificially but advance them "at will," units whose meaning could best be understood if they were likened to an "autocrat" or a "master."

So Sherman systematically imported the terminology of politics and of purposive action into his analysis of the trusts. Moreover, he saw the trusts as causing political problems other than that of marginally higher prices. When he first introduced his resolution, he asserted that popular opinion was coming to see the market power of trusts as a political issue of a fundamental sort. But furthermore, he objected to the trusts' relations with groups other than consumers—to the fact that they were able to "reach state authorities" and to the fact that they could also exercise disproportionate control over the producers of labor, over their own workers. The trusts, these views of Sherman's implied, were to be feared for more than threats to people in their role as consumers; the trusts also threatened the populace in its role as worker or citizen.[29]

One can easily see how a reader so inclined might dismiss these aspects of Sherman's speeches. One could view his statements about broader political consequences as merely ancillary to his major theme of the restraint of purely economic competition, and one could view his adjectives and metaphors as accidents, as embellishments that reveal nothing more than the character of the political rhetoric of the time and that add no distinctive concepts to his arguments.

But in the end it is hard to see why these "embellishing" words should be taken less seriously than the ones that carry a fairly precise meaning for modern economics. And if one does take seriously the manner in which Sherman expressed himself, one must conclude that he worried about market power not only for its potential threat to consumer welfare in the economic sense but also for its status as a species of personal and political power. The problem of the trusts was not merely a problem of consumer welfare, it was as well the problem of where power should reside in a liberal democracy. The trusts, by their market power, their absolute size, their illegitimate political activity, and their willfulness, posed the threat of a private force more powerful than the public one and sufficient to compromise the independence of individual citizens. Sherman's perception, in other words, was the popular perception that private power was to be mistrusted, that private power not subordinate to public power was a grave danger, and that the form of public control should, where possible, be such as to prohibit this species of political power rather than to legitimate it.

In its general form, this perception is by no means inconsistent with the desire to promote consumer welfare in a stricter economic sense; it would be inaccurate to impute to Sherman or his colleagues a well-developed alternative notion of the purposes of antitrust. But Sherman's association of economic power with purposively exercised political power suggests an antitrust attitude in one sense broader and in another sense narrower than that associated with a strictly economic approach. It is broader in the sense that it mistrusts private power for reasons in addition to those of economics; and it is at least potentially narrower because it tends to emphasize purposiveness as a crucial sign of the existence of this power.

There has been recent and well-taken criticism of the notion, so often apparent in the antitrust opinions handed down by the federal courts, that the Sherman Act meant to impose on American economic life a whole range of values, from the survival of small business to the freedom from fear, that are not only different from but sometimes inimical to the goal of maximizing economic welfare for the consumer; certainly there is nothing in the language of the act or the debates that would force one to conclude that the legislators had in mind values they thought contradictory to the goal of consumer welfare.[30] But Sherman did not speak entirely of economics, and he did not give clear indications of which of his desiderata were central to his scheme and which merely ancillary. He spoke a political language, one supporting several goals that he simply assumed to be compatible with one another; he was ambiguous about the relationships among them, and it is hardly surprising that in the course of the antitrust laws' application, these ambiguities have assumed a controlling force of their own.

If Sherman's idea of the nature of the trust problem remains in the end an ambiguous one, it is just as important that the method he supported for the enforcement of antitrust policy was one well suited to perpetuate the ambiguity. The Sherman Act prohibits "restraints of trade" and "monopolization"; it does not define its terms, and thus it leaves to the courts the matter of deciding what these terms shall mean. Though the act finally passed was not Sherman's original version, Sherman had used the term "restraints of trade" from the beginning of his project and he made clear why he had chosen to do so. The bill, he explained, "does not announce a new principle of law, but applies old and well-recognized principles of the common law to the complicated jurisdiction of our State and Federal government."[31] The offenses prohibited by his proposed law, Sherman went on to say, were already offenses under the common and statute law and could already be prosecuted in the state courts. The purposes of the new law were simply to ease the jurisdictional problems that hampered enforcement through the state courts and to establish clearly that the public—in this case, federal law enforcement officials—and not merely injured private parties could bring suit and impose penalties on the wrongdoers. Sherman repeated this view several times. The "single object" of the bill, he said, was "to invoke the aid of the courts of the United States to . . . supplement the enforcement of the common and statute law by the courts of the several States. . . . Now, Mr. President, what is this bill? A remedial statute to enforce by civil process in the courts of the United States the common law against monopolies."[32]

As Letwin points out, it is ironic that Sherman chose to emphasize the potential efficacy of the existing common law against restraints of trade.[33] It is true that the English common law, adopted in America as well, contained strictures against the crimes of "monopolies," "forestalling," "engrossing," "contracts in restraint of trade," and "combinations in restraint of trade." But it seems, to follow Letwin, that very few of the large trusts that Sherman appears to have had in mind could have been destroyed or even have had most of their objectionable practices controlled by an application of this common law, whether in its British or in its slightly more radical American form.

The English common law against monopolies, first of all, never had much influence as a precedent for American courts because it applied only to monopolies explicitly granted by the state. The common law against "engrossing," or cornering the supply of a commodity, had become practically extinct. The law against "contracts in restraint of trade"—that is, agreements by one party not to engage in competition with another—had been interpreted to permit even very broad restraints of this type provided those restraints were "reasonable"; and "reasonableness," as Thorelli says, had come to be judged by whether the parties making the agreement considered their contract reasonable. Finally, the law against "combinations in restraint of trade"—though American courts had in fact extended it to cover some mergers and other "tight" forms of combination, as opposed to simple agreements among otherwise independent producers on matters such as price-fixing or setting production quotas—was becoming increasingly lenient toward various forms of industrial combination.[34]

It seems unlikely that Sherman would have agreed with this modern analysis of the common law's applicability. The legal profession of his own time thought that the common law could indeed be used against many forms of loose and tight combination,[35] and Sherman certainly spoke at various points as if he thought so as well. Perhaps even more important, Sherman explicitly declared that his own particular view of the existing common law was irrelevant to the purposes he had in mind for his bill. "I admit," he responded to one criticism of his vagueness,[36]

that it is difficult to define in legal language the precise line between lawful and unlawful combinations. This must be left for the courts to determine in each particular case. All that we, as lawmakers, can do is to declare general principles, and we can be assured that the courts will apply them so as to carry out the meaning of the law. . . .

In short, Sherman did not consider it a grave embarrassment that he was unclear as to the type of combination or practice he intended to prohibit; instead, he was satisfied to look to the courts for eventual determination of the law's particular applications.

Sherman and Congress drew back, then, from the imposition of new, specific public standards on the conduct of business. Sherman lacked faith in the market to the extent that he thought some kind of public control over it necessary. But he stressed several times in his speeches the benefits that business had brought to America and he showed no desire to substitute explicitly political standards for market standards any more than he thought minimally necessary. In the same way, Congress chose as the vehicle for its antitrust policy not the already available model of the regulatory commission but the device of the courts and the common law, and the common law seems to have signified to the legislators not any specific set of substantive prescriptions but instead a form of decision making that seemed particularly suited to the aims of antitrust. The courts exhibited several characteristics—the ability to discriminate among particular cases, the particularistic mode of reasoning, the tendency toward incrementalism, the adversary system—that permitted the assertion of the principle of public control while minimizing the violence that control would do to the principle of private decision making in the economic sphere.

Congress chose, then, a form of enforcement that would by its nature limit the extent to which administrative decisions could by themselves determine antitrust matters. This choice had consequences for the future of antitrust enforcement. For one thing, it placed the final settlement of antitrust questions in a forum not likely to provide for the most definitive resolution of conflicts over the meaning of antitrust. For another, it placed final decisions beyond the unilateral control of the executive branch of the federal government, not only in theory but in common practice. To put it another way, the executive's antitrust personnel were created as prosecutors rather than judges.[37]

As the introductory chapter asserted and as the following chapters will try to show, the present-day Antitrust Division reflects in many ways the spirit and ambiguities of the congressional intention. But it has often been pointed out that antitrust enforcement and its organization have by no means been uniform over time in their vigor or in the policies that have guided them. Part of this fluctuation, it is said, stems from the state of the antitrust case law at any particular time; another major part is said to depend on the political opinions and partisan connections of various national administrations. Both these alleged factors do of course have their effects on antitrust enforcement, but there is some reason to ask just how large these effects have been.

Antitrust enforcement, we have been reminded, got off to a slow start. Between the years 1890 and 1904, the government brought an average of fewer than 1.5 antitrust cases per year.[38] This initial inactivity has been explained in several ways.[39] Some of the early attorneys general in charge of antitrust enforcement were personally antagonistic toward the Sherman Act. And even had these attorneys general been enthusiastic about it, there would still have remained their uncertainty as to whether the law was constitutional at all and whether it could possibly be interpreted in such a way as to make it an effective and important sanction against then-current objectionable business practices and organization. Finally, in the early years of enforcement there was simply no special appropriation granted to the Justice Department for antitrust purposes. The entire department, at the time, consisted of only eighteen lawyers already heavily burdened with other types of cases, and attorneys general therefore had to rely for information and prosecutorial efforts mainly on the individual preferences and energies of a group of highly independent U.S. attorneys.

The first significant increase in the number of antitrust prosecutions came not with President Theodore Roosevelt's highly publicized attack on the Northern Securities Company in 1901 but instead only after Roosevelt and Attorney General Philander Knox had persuaded Congress to grant the department its first appropriation for the specific purpose of antitrust enforcement, an amount of five hundred thousand dollars to be expended over a period of five years. This appropriation, granted in 1904, enabled the department to hire five full-time antitrust lawyers[40]— a number that, in light of the department's overall size, did not reflect unfavorably on the seriousness of Congress's antitrust intentions. The number of prosecutions by the government thereafter increased significantly; the average number of cases brought per year for 1905 through 1909 was almost eight.[41] During the years 1910 through 1914, the number of prosecutions reached an average of thirty-one per year, a level that was not to be attained again until the late 1930s.[42]

In 1915, despite an additional increase in the number of antitrust staff lawyers to eighteen,[43] the number of prosecutions fell to the level of seven per year;[44] and the number of cases remained low—about eleven cases a year—throughout the 1920s. The ready explanation for this drop is that President Wilson during World War I, followed by the business-oriented administrations of the 1920s, simply gave orders that certain antitrust cases were not to be brought. Without an exhaustive examination of the records of the period, it is impossible to come to a clear verdict on this hypothesis; a reading of the department's general correspondence files on antitrust through the 1920s, and a fragmentary examination of some industry files, have not revealed the direct evidence to support it, though these bodies of information do not constitute the complete record.[45] Indeed, the most striking impression one gains from various investigation files is of the similarity between the concerns and procedures of antitrust lawyers of that period and those described by their present-day counterparts. But the low level of cases actually brought by the government did persist until Franklin Roosevelt's decision to sanction industrywide cooperation through the National Industrial Recovery Act brought the annual number of prosecutions to a still lower level, about six per year. This figure was the lowest since Congress had begun granting the special antitrust appropriation in 1904.[46]

The downward trend was reversed abruptly in 1938, when, after the NIRA had been declared unconstitutional, Roosevelt was persuaded to reinvigorate antitrust enforcement as a substitute for the National Recovery Administration in controlling big business.[47] The agent of this reinvigoration was Thurman Arnold, who that year became the new assistant attorney general in charge of the Antitrust Division and served in the post until 1943. When Arnold arrived the division's budget was increased to about eight hundred thousand dollars, the number of lawyers increased over the course of only one year from 59 to 144,[48] a small staff of economists was added to the division for the first time, vastly more publicity was generated concerning the division's activities,[49] the number of complaints processed rose significantly, and the number of cases brought rose suddenly to over fifty per year, the highest level in division history.[50] Corwin D. Edwards has both described these aspects of Arnold's tenure at the Antitrust Division and told of Arnold's program of concerted attacks on anticompetitive practices in specific industries;[51] it was the organizational and policy changes Arnold made, it is widely believed, that marked the birth of the modern Antitrust Division.

It is important to know what kind of organization Arnold found waiting for him when he arrived, precisely how he tried to change it, and what kind of organization he left behind him. The most concise picture we have of the pre-Arnold division comes from a seminar that Arnold himself organized in 1938, after he had first arrived, to acquaint the influx of new personnel with both the division's ongoing procedures and the changes that the new regime had begun making in these procedures.[52] Two of the lectures in this seminar described the ways in which the division customarily received information and the way it dealt with this information once received; Arnold did not propose to make major alterations in either of these aspects of the organization.[53]

The division, it was explained, received most of its information from complaints, most of which came from small businessmen annoyed at the practices of their suppliers or competitors. The following were presented as typical examples: a Washington lawyer complaining that when he had tried to trade in his typewriter for a new one, all the stores he had gone to had quoted him identical trade-in and new-machine prices; a lawyer complaining that a large company was forcing his client out of business; a jobber complaining that he was being boycotted by all his suppliers. Each of these complaints was handled by a lawyer who made a preliminary study of the industry involved from library materials, division files, financial manuals, newspapers, and trade journals. If the lawyer decided the complaint was worthwhile he would begin a field investigation, perhaps calling on the Federal Bureau of Investigation for aid.

Arnold and his staff did not criticize this general procedure, but they were indeed critical of other aspects of previous practice.[54] For one thing, too many cases were being settled by consent decrees; henceforth there would be fewer such settlements. Too many prosecutions were being brought as civil rather than criminal cases; the balance would now be redressed. And there were simply not enough cases being brought; so the division would henceforth bring more, and Arnold's reorganization would enable the lawyers to do so.

This reorganization would be of several kinds. For one thing, the old division was inefficient in bringing cases because as the number of complaints had increased, the division had continued its old policy of investigating everything in detail and had thus wasted its time on what turned out to be fruitless investigations. (One may speculate that this practice may have contributed to the low number of cases brought during the 1920s.) Now there was to be a new complaints section, separate from the investigative and trial staffs, whose job would be to screen all the incoming complaints, to garner as much information as possible by mail instead of by personal visit, and thus to enable the division to be more efficient in its decisions about which complaints were to be accepted for field investigation. In other words, explained the speaker, describing the planned change, the new section was "to reduce the ratio of field investigations to complaints" and thus ensure the best possible use of the division's limited resources.[55]

The second major aspect of division investigations that Arnold proposed to change was the lawyers' particularism and their failure to think of antitrust enforcement in objective, systematic, economic terms. The lawyers were too exclusively concerned with the actual, current behavior of business firms and with winning the case at hand, not concerned enough with the economic impact of their work. To remedy this defect, Arnold had established a new economics section. No longer would a lawyer be totally on his own in the preparation of cases that promised to have a large economic impact. From now on, if the lawyer decided that a complaint looked like a potential case and that the case looked important economically, he could call not only on the FBI for investigative help but on the economics section as well. The economics section would investigate the whole industry of which the complaint was a part, not only to provide buttressing facts and arguments to the lawyer in making the case at hand but also to identify other possible points for attack.[56]

So Arnold was making two kinds of criticism of the old division. First, it was not vigorous enough in applying the law's maximum penalties. This he would change with his new policies of increasing the number of criminal prosecutions and decreasing the number of consent decrees. Second, the division had been too particularistic, too concerned with the case at hand, too prone to ignore potential economic impact as a criterion for investigation. This he would change with the new complaints section and economics section; they would help the division bring not only more cases but more economically important cases.

When observers examined the Antitrust Division shortly after the end of Arnold's tenure, they found that in some ways he had indubitably been successful, made good on his promises, and changed the division. More criminal cases were indeed brought, fewer were settled by consent decree, and the publicity accompanying these cases is widely accepted as having increased not only the number of complaints but also the quality of the preliminary information the division had at its disposal. So Arnold made good on those aspects of his criticism that called attention to the division's general level of activity and vigor.[57]

But it is not so clear that Arnold changed what he saw as an equally basic flaw in the division—its particularistic, behavior-oriented, economically unsystematic pattern of enforcement. First, there is the question of exactly how Arnold was able to increase the overall number of antitrust prosecutions—of whether the increase was in fact due to the lawyers' using their investigative time and energies more efficiently. Lawyers who went to the division at the same time that Arnold arrived suggest some other explanations for the rise in activity. First, there was simply the tremendous increase in the number of division lawyers. Second, these then-young men worked very hard out of the sense of excitment Arnold promoted. Third, it is said that the period that had immediately preceded Arnold, the period of government-sanctioned, industrywide collusion on prices, output, and practices under the National Industrial Recovery Act had left a huge residue of easily obtained evidence that could be used in cases involving the continuation of these collusive practices. The laxness of enforcement during the NIRA period had made businessmen careless about concealing illegal dealings; and not only had the NIRA made such evidence easier to get, it had also actually promoted collusion where none had existed before. "You have to remember," one of Arnold's protégés in the division explained of that period, "that those cases were easy. The evidence was just lying around waiting for someone to pick it up. You don't get cases like that any more." In short, they brought more cases in no small part because there were simply more good cases lying around to be brought.

Just as important, it is not clear that the new complaints section had much effect on the criteria by which the lawyers selected their investigations. As its section head described the procedures that the new section had begun to follow, someone might complain that a company's salesman had quoted a price that represented unfair price discrimination. A letter to the company, rather than a visit, might produce a denial that the salesman had in fact been authorized to quote that price, and in the absence of further evidence the complaint could be dropped and a lawyer's field investigative time saved. Or, the section head went on, the offense complained of might be a rule of a particular trade association. If an inquiry to the association resulted in an immediate change in the offending rule, that could be the end of the matter.[58]

What is interesting about these examples is that they reveal criteria of decision that were no different from, and did not purport to be different from, those used by the Justice Department of 1910 or 1923. There is nothing in these examples to suggest that the complaints section was going to apply rules different from those trial lawyers themselves would have applied; there is nothing to indicate that the new section intended to change either the definition of a violation or the ways of getting evidence of one.

This is not to say that a change such as this did not save the lawyers' time for other, possibly more important, things. But Arnold had criticized the division not only for its logistical inefficiency but for its lack of selectivity. He implied that his new device for processing complaints would bear on both these problems, but in fact it did not introduce any new substantive criteria for choosing among complaints. Arnold's new complaints section simply permitted the already existing principles of selection to be applied at an earlier stage of investigation—an important change in itself, but only half of what he had in mind.

A similar comment can be made about the new economics section that Arnold instituted. It is true that the section was used a great deal by the division's lawyers in broadening their cases to include larger portions of the various industries they were investigating. But the economics section was an aid used at the lawyers' discretion; it did not initiate actions independently. And even within this limited sphere, its role was a very special one. One staff member described an example that he took to imply that the economics section was introducing new criteria into the selection of cases. In one instance, he said, the price of a certain commodity seemed to have been fixed. But the economics section, asked for its opinion, pointed out that the structure of the industry was such that uniform prices might have been expected without collusion. The lawyer involved was advised that price figures alone, without other kinds of evidence, did not warrant the investment of major investigative resources.[59]

This kind of advice was useful, but it was of a very limited nature. It was an advance of sorts for the lawyer in question to learn something more about the connection between industry structure and price uniformity; but the economics section, rather than playing an independent role in deciding where the division should put its resources, was simply giving this lawyer a faster way to determine whether he would probably find what he would have been looking for in any case. The economics section is reported to have been a valuable tool for Arnold's lawyers, but it made no attempt to change the organization's fundamental perception of its mission. Again, the new section was part of a significant change, but the change was only half of what Arnold had announced.

One reason why the new sections did not introduce new principles of decision is suggested by the speech that yet another of Arnold's top staff members made to new recruits. The reason that the division had to become more discriminating about its cases and more conscious of the economic impact of these cases, it was explained, was that there simply weren't enough lawyers to investigate everything. But in his next sentence, the speaker noted that this personnel shortage was being significantly "mitigated" by the new and larger appropriations that had just been made available to the division.[60] Thus, at the same time Arnold was trying to wean the division from its ad hoc methods of prosecution, the increase in personnel was making it less necessary for the organization to make those choices that Arnold's vision of it would have required.

Arnold succeeded in changing the division in some ways but failed in others. Where it was a question of increasing penalties or expanding the number of prosecutions, he did well enough—as, in various areas, it will be seen that future assistant attorneys general would also do. Arnold succeeded in other ways as well—in making investigative procedures more efficient, in building the division to a size that encouraged a routinely higher level of division activity, and in generating a type of publicity that improved the quality of the information available to the organization and that may have had a deterrent effect. But the internal evidence indicates that he did not succeed in imposing a system to replace the existing case-by-case, court-oriented method of antitrust enforcement.

This was also the verdict of some of the best-known outside observers of Arnold's division. In 1940, Walton Hamilton and Irene Till made a study of the division for the Temporary National Economic Commission. Hamilton and Till criticized antitrust enforcement for its lack of continuity—a criticism that must have seemed particulary cogent when one was comparing Arnold's regime with that of his immediate predecessors under the NIRA. It was therefore advisable, Hamilton and Till said, to re-form the division as an independent commission.[61]

But if the authors found a disturbing discontinuity in antitrust enforcement, they were even more disturbed by a pattern in its behavior that made it difficult for outsiders to impose new directions on the organization. The crucial limitation lay in the fact that the division's professionals were largely lawyers who practiced "The Lawyer's Approach to Antitrust":[62]

. . . the way of the law pervades the work of Antitrust. . . . The task could probably be best served by an amphibian who could use with equal ease the idiom of law and economics. Yet . . . the character of . . . investigation is determined by the Division's obligation to prosecute. . . . The Antitrust attorney seizes whatever is helpful, discards whatever might tell against him. . . . He gathers evidence instead of finding facts. . . . The grand total at which he arrives is far more a recitation of wrongdoing than a picture of an industry at work. . . . The attorneys develop zeal in their work, are persuaded of the guilt of the accused, bend every effort that the breach of the law shall be atoned. . . . An Economics Section has been organized but such units tend to be excrescences upon a structure which has made little place for them. They are not easily woven into litigation which is the principle activity of the Division.

Arnold had made similar criticisms of the division, and while he may have increased his lawyers' "zeal in their work," he presided over an organization that, to judge by Hamilton and Till's verdict, was similar to the one he had taken over in crucial respects. It was an organization marked by an attention to particular cases, by a certain zeal in prosecution, by a discomfort with the idea of setting forth a detailed or comprehensive policy posture toward the economy as a whole, by a tendency to resolve ambiguities through legal craftsmanship. It may not have been the organization that John Sherman and the Congress of 1890 would have wanted, but it is hard to say that it was greatly worse than they deserved.

3
The Prosecutors

The present-day Antitrust Division reflects to a striking degree the spirit and ambiguities of the legislation it was created to enforce, and one can see this reflection first of all in the careers and operational routines of the division's professional personnel. Because the antitrust laws are enforced in the courts, the division's task calls for the skills of lawyers. It does not necessarily call for lawyers in the high proportion in which they are present; one can conceive of more of the division's work being performed by economists, by nonprofessional but specially trained field investigators, by accountants, or by professional negotiators. But the division has never undertaken any such elaborate division of labor. The organization does have economists, and their numbers are increasing;[1] and it does use the Federal Bureau of Investigation to perform some of the more routine parts of its investigations. But overwhelmingly the division hires lawyers.

Joining the Division

When one inquires into staff members' motives for joining the division, one is first struck by the importance of their ages. At the time of this study, there was a remarkably clear distinction in the division between younger lawyers and older lawyers. To judge from the sample of attorneys interviewed, there were about a dozen staff lawyers in the division between the ages of thirty-five and fifty. About two-thirds of the remaining Antitrust staff lawyers were under thirty-five years old, and about one-third was fifty or older.[2] And the two extreme groups—under thirty-five and fifty or above —came to the division under markedly different circumstances.

The older lawyers may be described more briefly because their motives involved relatively little calculation about, concern over, the division's function. Some of the oldest went to the division, it is true, because of Thurman Arnold and the glamour and excitement he created; but others of this generation, especially those from the South, went to work for Arnold simply because the expanding division provided some of the few jobs available to young lawyers during the late depression. Some joined because they had friends in the division who encouraged them to join; some joined because they had applied to a large number of public agencies and private firms and simply received their first or best offer from Antitrust. A number of lawyers, slightly younger, arrived just after World War II, when the wartime agencies for which they had been working were disbanded. But whatever the particulars of their cases, the persistent theme in the accounts given by the older lawyers is the absence of any special attraction to the idea of antitrust itself or, except for some of those who joined in the Arnold era, to any broader rationale for antitrust enforcement. In response to the standard question about how they came to their present jobs, the division's older lawyers would overwhelmingly begin with a smile or an ironic chuckle and go on to say, "Actually, it was an accident," or "Well, you might say I just fell into it," or some other introduction calling attention to the role of chance in their decisions.

These older lawyers are about equally divided between those who joined the division intending to leave soon and those who intended to make their careers in government. About half of them, particularly the oldest among them and those who mentioned the depression in their accounts, said that they had set their sights on government careers and never had any intention of leaving the federal service. About an equal number said that they had stayed by accident, just as they had joined by accident. They went to Antitrust planning to leave it eventually for more lucrative private work. Sometimes, it seems evident, the opportunity to leave never came. Just as frequently, though, an older lawyer pointed to an opportunity that did materialize but was rejected because he had become engrossed in each of the long cases that followed one another in his career and had decided that private practice could never offer work of comparable interest.

The younger lawyers displayed a much more uniform set of motives for having applied to the division. These young attorneys graduated from law school in the late 1950s or afterwards. The time of graduation is important for two reasons. First of all, in 1955, Attorney General Herbert Brownell changed the Justice Department's hiring procedures. Before 1955, young lawyers had all been hired "off the street," as one division administrator put it. To replace this method, or at least curtail its use, Brownell instituted the Attorney General's Honors Program, which now provides the majority of the department's new professional personnel.[3] The first requirement for admission under the new program is that an applicant stand in the top 10 percent of his or her law school class. The program chooses from among the applicants by sending top officials from the department's various legal divisions and the attorney general's office to visit the participating law schools, evaluate the candidates, and persuade especially desirable ones to join the Justice Department.

Under the honors program, an applicant may name his first three choices among the department's divisions. Some effort is made to equalize the quality of new lawyers in the various divisions: The recruiters rank all candidates on a common list, and if candidates ranked one through twenty-five all want to go to to the Lands Division, they will not all get there. But the distribution of preferences among the candidates is such that there have been almost no new lawyers hired for Antitrust under the honors program who have not named the division as their first choice.

A major consequence of this hiring procedure is that the candidates interviewed are bright and are perceived as being very bright. The most desirable ones are viewed as valuable commodities who are to be wooed to the department, though the precise amount of wooing required varies with the state of the general job market for young attorneys. One of the inducements offered is that if a successful applicant decides to join the department, he will get a lot of experience in a very short time. Young division lawyers hired through the honors program mentioned repeatedly that this argument had been made to them and that the argument is an effective one; the candidates themselves want very much to gain a fund of experience that they can use later to obtain jobs in private practice.

The second reason why it is significant that these young lawyers graduated in or after the late 1950s, whether they got to the division through the honors program or by some other route, is that the fifties saw a considerable increase in antitrust activity by both the government and the private antitrust bar. The antimerger provisions of the Clayton Act had been amended in 1950, bringing a large number of mergers newly within the reach of the division, and eventually the division exploited this expanded jurisdiction.[4] Further, in 1957, business executives were for the first time actually forced to serve jail sentences under the Sherman Act;[5] and in 1959, the government brought an indictment against the country's major manufacturers of heavy electrical equipment in one of the biggest and most highly publicized price-fixing cases in American history.[6]

It would not be fair to interpret these events as evidence that antitrust was becoming a popular political cause again, or one that might significantly change the nature of Antitrust recruits by making antitrust enforcement glamorous again to a new generation of lawyers. But what these events did do was to make antitrust expertise a more valuable commodity to the business community and to law firms serving it. Private lawyers remember the time in the late fifties when the demand for antitrust counsel began to be felt: "All of a sudden they started coming in the door asking us if they were doing anything illegal, asking us to help them start compliance programs. They were scared." This new demand in the private bar for antitrust expertise eventually came to include a demand for lawyers who had served in the division itself, not only because of their presumed familiarity with the antitrust law but also because of their presumed knowledge of the division's preferences and operating routines.[7]

The consequence of this increased demand was that experience in the Antitrust Division became newly valuable to a young lawyer who wanted eventually to work in private practice, as it turned out to be valuable to those who had arrived in the division before the antitrust boom and who already had considerable experience by the time it occurred. But it was especially valuable to the young lawyers applying to the division under the honors program. Though these are people of some ability, they are also people for whom the government experience will be a valuable asset in seeking eventual employment in the private sector.[8] These young attorneys ranked not quite at the top of their classes at the most highly rated law schools or nearer the top of schools not so well placed. There are of course individual exceptions, but most of these recruits said that they could significantly improve their chances for a successful private career by adding to their law school records a specific skill such as the one the Antitrust Division teaches. These are the recruits who both qualify for and are attracted to jobs in the Antitrust Division.

The consequence of this set of motives and circumstances is that what these young attorneys want from the Antitrust Division is the experience and skills they think they will need to recommend them in their future careers. As one of them described his thinking, "I liked trial work and government is the place to get experience. . . . After a while I'll go into private practice. . . . Now the job market is lousy—but there *is* a network of information about these things. Even if you're not going into antitrust, the experience is a good selling point. . . . If you get a reputation for being good, the firms will hear." And another put it more simply: "Government is a good start for future practice. You need to know how government operates."

When these young attorneys say they want experience, they do not mean that they want to improve their skill in legal research. Instead, they say they came to the division wanting skills of a more practical kind. They want to learn about the division's operating procedures—the considerations that "really" influence the choice of particular antitrust cases, aside from the considerations they may already have gleaned from court opinions. They want to learn about the practical details of the investigation and preparation of cases—not only how and when to complete the various formal steps but how to use documents, interrogatories, interviews, and other investigative tools for developing evidence in a case. They want to learn something of the style of antitrust lawyers. And most important, they want courtroom experience, and experience more specifically in the federal courts. "I was looking for a place to get litigating experience quickly" was an often-made explanation, and, as one young lawyer put it, "In the Antitrust Division, you're dealing with the federal courts—stuff that'll be useful to you whatever you go into."

Many of these lawyers, therefore, said that they would not have considered government work for an administrative agency; direct experience with the federal courts was a major attraction. They said that they had not been aware before coming to the division of the extreme length of antitrust cases in their preparation for trial, the small proportion of complaints investigated that seem worthy of prosecution, or the small proportion of cases filed that ever reach the courtroom. They think that trial experience is crucial to their reputations; in this it seems that they exaggerate, but it is their opinion nevertheless.

By contrast, promotion within the division seems of relatively little concern to them. They prefer more money to less money and value their early promotions as a sign of the general regard in which they are held, but most of the lawyers who have entered the division since the honors program began have left it well before the time they would become eligible for the pay and responsibility accorded to the organization's most senior lawyers, and most of the young lawyers interviewed express their intention to do the same.

So there are considerations of personal advantage that bring young lawyers to the division. But one should not make too much of the extent to which they chose the Antitrust Division merely from such considerations. It is safe to say that few of them would be there were this experience not at least compatible with their desired future careers. But there are other divisions in the Justice Department—the Tax Division, for instance—that bestow comparable advantages on their personnel. And almost all the young lawyers in the Antitrust Division chose Antitrust over the other divisions out of a deliberate preference for dealing with antitrust law itself.

There are two reasons they give for this preference. One is simply that antitrust law seems to them more intellectually interesting than comparable law specialties. The antitrust laws seem broadly enough drawn to permit a certain amount of creativity in interpretation. Because of the law's breadth and its obvious connection with large social and economic questions, it gives one, some young lawyers say, a sense of participation in important issues. There is no doubt that these young lawyers in the Antitrust Division value very highly the opportunity to become experts without having to descend to what they consider the status of technicians. Several lawyers remarked specifically that they had chosen the Antitrust Division over the Tax Division because they had wanted to become specialists; they considered Tax and Antitrust the two main places in which they could fulfill this goal, but they could not bring themselves to "bury" themselves "in the nitpicking tax code."

The second reason these lawyers prefer Antitrust—a reason given with greater frequency by new arrivals—is a negative one. To them, Antitrust is one of the few law practices, aside from the more patently idealistic callings of civil rights or consumer or environmental law, they think "honorable." They use the word "honorable" in more than one sense. First, many state explicity that their aversion to a field like tax law as a permanent specialty stems not only from its technical nature but from their eventual unwillingness to defend individuals against what they consider to be the public interest. Further, when they speak of making their own future careers in the private antitrust bar, they invariably emphasize their intention not to "sell out" to their clients—and they think that the antitrust field permits one to avoid such compromises. There is nothing impious about their references to their future careers, not much cynicism about reversing the ends to which their skills will be put. "There's creditable work to be done in the defense bar," one young lawyer put it. Another explained, "Most of the work you do for them [private clients] will be preventive—telling them what they *can't* do."

They make similar moral distinctions when comparing antitrust enforcement with other kinds of law practice within the federal government. Several said that they chose Antitrust over other government jobs because they wanted a job in which being a government advocate would almost invariably mean being on the "right" side. One lawyer had transferred into Antitrust from the Civil Division of the Justice Department because he was tired, as he put it, of "defending the government against widows and orphans trying to collect their Social Security benefits." And some of the younger lawyers chose Antitrust as the one Justice Department division they saw as being relatively immune from the perversion of goals the Nixon administration was presumed to have visited upon the rest of the department. They thought that Antitrust, at least, had not had its goals or basic methods of operation made less acceptable. Antitrust remained a place where one could practice law in good conscience.

The young lawyers, then, thought of antitrust as an "honorable" field in two senses—in the sense that their government work in antitrust would place them on the "right" side and in the sense that they could somehow transfer their skills to private practice without automatically joining the "wrong" side. But just as important is what these lawyers' motives and expectations were not. It is true that they were looking for a calling of which they would not be ashamed, a job whose contribution to the public interest was self-evident and would not have to be explained or argued for or rationalized. But few of them, it appeared, had seriously considered those jobs that during their school years were most closely associated with the young, socially conscious lawyer. For instance, few said that they had listed the Civil Rights Division as one of their choices on their honors program applications. And while one could argue that some might have joined Civil Rights had it not been for a disillusionment with the government's civil rights policies, neither do most of them seem to have thought seriously of the "public interest" law firms or of comparable government-sponsored legal aid projects. In other words, they seem to want an occupation that prevailing liberal norms mark as honorable, but they have not associated themselves with the organizations embodying the most fashionable recent liberal causes. This piece of evidence suggests what will later be described in more detail—that there is an important difference between these lawyers' more general attitudes toward their chosen task and those of the lawyers one might expect to find staffing the organizations that more clearly embody the major social concerns of recent years.

The division's older lawyers, then, came into the division for a variety of motives, most of which can be termed "accidental" to the particular purposes of or the personal benefits to be derived from antitrust enforcement as such. Some of them planned to stay in government service and might therefore be expected to have developed a special concern for promotion within the division and for those values and modes of behavior conducive to rising through the hierarchy; just as many did not plan to stay, and many of these decided to stay because they liked the jobs they already had. The younger lawyers, we have seen, went to the division because they were looking for a calling that was both personally beneficial and unambiguously respectable. They do not plan, by and large, to stay with the division and they seem to have relatively little concern with internal promotion. These sets of motives suggest one important feature of the division: that if there is any significant degree of uniformity of style and attitudes among the staff, the mechanism for control and socialization is not simply the organization's formal reward structure. But these motives do not suggest much about what the nature of such uniformities actually might be or what the mechanism of socialization actually is. To get some idea of these, one must ask another set of questions about the lawyers' opinions.

The Lawyers' Commitment

One striking uniformity among the staff lawyers is the relative absence among them of attitudes one associates with the zealot or the thoroughgoing ideologue. This absence is apparent when one questions the lawyers, both younger and older, about their opinions of the importance of their own work and the division's larger task. The first thing one discovers through such questioning is how difficult it is to elicit from them any statement of a general kind on the subject of antitrust. The lawyers are forthcoming and will talk spontaneously and at length about their own careers, about their opinions of decisions made by the higher echelons, and especially about their own cases. But they do not seem accustomed to making broader judgments about the present state or proper role of antitrust enforcement.

First of all, there is no consensus on the morally crucial question of why businessmen violate the antitrust laws. One young lawyer, to be sure, when asked about his opponents' motives, answered quite readily that businessmen fix prices in full knowledge of their wrongdoing, "and for good Marxist reasons—to establish a joint monopoly and make maximum profits." But such reasoning was by no means typical. By far the majority of the staff lawyers would not so simply attribute foreknowledge or willfulness—not to speak of evil—to antitrust violators.

One might argue that this finding is anything but surprising: Antitrust cases, after all, often turn on legal interpretations that are by no means obvious even to the prosecuting attorneys, let alone judges, juries, or defendants. But the same attitude held even when lawyers were speaking of cases of unambiguous price-fixing. "These guys just didn't know what they were doing," one lawyer reminisced about a past price-fixing case. "It was a kind of family tradition, meeting every so often to decide on the price of _____ in the _____ area. It wasn't as if they were particularly *high* prices, compared to other cities—and they simply didn't know they were doing anything wrong." Another lawyer remembered one incident in which he had been called to a businessmen's meeting to hear a complaint of theirs about a possible antitrust violation by a competing group. "We all met in a motel room," he said,

and we [the Antitrust Division lawyers] discussed their complaint with them. Then, as the meeting broke up and we were all leaving, they started a casual discussion about what the price of _____ should be for the next six months or so. Right in *front* of us! We had to tell them, "Hey, at least wait till we're out of the room!" These guys—not the industrial giants, but the little guys—don't know it's something wrong.

To be sure, in their actual pursuit of investigations, the staff lawyers often exhibit a highly developed mistrust of their opponents' good faith. But, as we shall see, this skepticism comes more from the structure of the adversary proceeding than from more fundamental attitudes toward the character of businessmen. The skepticism is most pronounced with regard to those opponents—the larger businesses—whose violations are the *least* clear. In other words, the lawyers' knowledge of the circumstances under which antitrust violations can occur dissuades them from holding any consistent views about the moral turpitude of their adversaries.

If the lawyers are not driven by consistent feelings of moral outrage toward individual defendants, neither do they have any very complete view of antitrust's relation to the various social and economic goals that antitrust enforcement is often said to promote. This is not to say that these lawyers as a whole can fairly be described as "bureaucrats" in the pejorative sense of the word—that they have largely separated the performance of their day-to-day tasks from the goals for which that performance was intended, that they accept with few questions the constraints upon that performance, that they habitually seek the narrowest and easiest way of

fulfilling their duties, or that they are blind to all conflicting considerations of public interest in their prosecution of individual cases.
People of course exist in the division who are fairly subject to all
these criticisms; the complaint about "dead wood" is no more
absent there than it is in other organizations. But the division is
striking for the number of lawyers it supports, amid their less
imaginative colleagues, in their efforts to find ways of applying
laws to situations where they have never been applied or to bring
within the division's reach a set of facts that fall into no clear category of violation but that just "don't feel right" to an individual staff
lawyer.

Neither is this to say that the lawyers are unaware of the large and
persuasive body of economic writing that supports the worth of
the antitrust laws' contribution to desirable social and economic
goals. The point is, rather, that, in comparison to their comments
about narrower legal matters or individual cases, the lawyers' arguments about the social and economic benefits of antitrust are
remarkably vague and conflicting—one might almost call them
opportunistic.

One exception was the lawyer who said that he knew full well
that in some specific cases antitrust prosecution had arguably de-
creased the economic efficiency of the industry in question and
that not every merger he had opposed had violated the standards
of optimal efficiency. Nevertheless, he said, he was willing to sacrifice some economic efficiency because of his firm belief in the social and political virtues of an unconcentrated economy. Leaving
aside the merits of this argument, it can at least be said that this
lawyer had a relatively clear view of the trade-offs he was willing to
make in pursuit of his own general antitrust goals.

This way of thinking about antitrust enforcement, its social role,
and its costs was simply not very apparent throughout the rest of
the division's staff. Antitrust enforcement was said by them to lower prices, increase employment, improve the quality of goods and
services available to the consumer, and in general help to bring
about every desired condition in the economy—to say nothing of
the contribution it was claimed to make to the preservation of
democratic rule and individual liberty. Yet arguments purporting
to show that antitrust enforcement in a particular case may not

have contributed to one of those desired goals were met with a striking lack of concern.

Antitrust staffers concerned with the communications industry, for instance, were offered, for the purposes of argument, the hypothesis that monopoly may in fact be conducive to the production of a top-quality newspaper. The argument provoked not debate but simple skepticism and lack of interest. One extremely intelligent antitrust lawyer was asked what he thought of a recent action by another agency, in which a "procompetitive" decision had caused a major American city to lose one of its competing newspapers; he replied simply that a newspaper that existed by virtue of cross-subsidization didn't deserve to exist at all. Prosecutors of business concerns in one-company towns with relatively immobile labor forces were asked about the danger of creating unemployment. Sometimes the answer was simply that a company could not be believed when it predicted such dire results from antitrust action, but more often a lawyer would simply reply that antitrust enforcement was not responsible for the state of the economy as a whole. A similar pattern of response followed questions about efficiency: While maintaining that antitrust enforcement contributed to economic efficiency, lawyers would concede that in a particular case efficiency might have suffered yet feel their judgment had been correct when they had recommended prosecuting the case. There was rarely any mention of a conscious trade-off between competing values.

It is not that it was impossible, in each of these instances, to make a persuasive argument in favor of the antitrust opinion or prosecution being discussed, and it is certainly not that it is impossible to make the more general arguments in favor of the political or economic rationality of antitrust. What is at issue is not whether antitrust is good for our society; the point of note is rather that the lawyers seemed to have little interest in making these arguments at length, in much detail, or with much care to be right in the particular instance. They seemed to approach their economic and social arguments somewhat as they did their statements on the Antitrust Division's moral respectability: They were confident that the consensus supported them, they might well not have been in the division had that consensus not existed, they used such arguments as much as was necessary for what they thought of as success in their work—and that exhausted their interest in the matter. In other words, the hypothesis of moral zealotry or ideological commitment does not describe the staff's attitude toward its work. Asking questions based on these hypotheses produces relatively uniform responses: One finds that the lawyers do not express much of a personal animus or moral contempt toward their opponents, even though—or perhaps because—they work within a relatively formalized adversary context. One also finds that though they believe their work makes general social and economic sense, they seem not to be abashed or even much interested by competing social or economic arguments.

These are negative findings: They do not constitute a description of the principles the lawyers *do* bring to bear in their work. In fact there are such principles: They are the goals and norms of the prosecuting attorney.

The Ethos of Prosecution

If one asks the lawyers for a very general definition of their role —"What do you think your job in the division is or should be?"— one answer appears more than any other, and often in the same words: "My job" (—or "Our job"—) "is to enforce the antitrust laws." The statement is made with deliberate baldness and a certain well-controlled pride. It is made with similar frequency by old antitrust lawyers and by young people schooled in economics and fresh from economically oriented antitrust courses at law school. The lawyers make their declaration with the same sense of security evident in their pronouncements on the division's moral status and its economic respectability. They are sure that the consensus of opinion is in their favor and are not inclined to pursue the matter in detail. This "enforcement" definition of their role is the only one the lawyers offer spontaneously and without prompting.

It is a response, a conception of task, that seems by its simplicity to separate the lawyers' job not only from personal animus but even from a comprehensive reckoning of social and economic consequences. Yet it is a professional self-definition that requires further investigation, for a commitment to law enforcement certainly leaves room for widely varying notions of what that enforcement should entail. In the case of the division attorneys, it is possible to discover something about their shared attitudes toward enforcement by looking in detail at those few staff lawyers whom their colleagues especially admire and emulate.

There is substantial agreement among the division staff about who the exemplary members of the organization are, whose is the division's archetypal style, and who is worthy of emulation. One can be more precise about this: When one asks a division lawyer who *he* thinks is a good antitrust lawyer, the answer almost invariably includes one of a dozen names. Now this uniformity obviously does not mean that other attorneys as well are not admired by their fellows. But only a few men and one woman were widely and spontaneously mentioned not only as objects of admiration but as lawyers whom "you can really learn something from." Each section tends to have its own favorites, and a new lawyer is specially prone to mention the more senior attorney who was his first supervisor on a case. But among those who have been in the organization long enough to know of lawyers outside their own sections, the status of each "star" is recognized throughout.

This consensus is important because younger lawyers' attitudes toward and practice of enforcement are so heavily formed through emulation of their senior colleagues. Much of the division's work, though less of it than once was, is still organized on an apprentice system, with younger lawyers beginning their careers by helping older lawyers on various cases. Given the younger lawyers' reasons for being in the division in the first place, their desire to gain practical skills and experience, it is not surprising that they would be quite willing to learn from their senior supervising lawyers what the proper modes of behavior and reasoning are in an antitrust lawyer and to model themselves accordingly. But the fact that the older lawyers themselves share ideas about who the models are means that the transmission of attitudes and decision criteria to the younger attorneys does not depend wholly on the idiosyncrasies of the particular senior lawyers they happen to come into personal contact with. The older lawyers, as well as the younger attorneys who may have had no personal experience with their most widely admired colleagues, come to have a common notion of what the best antitrust lawyers take their job to be and how they perform it.

These most admired attorneys are of course lawyers of some experience in the division. They fall disproportionately into the underpopulated category of thirty-five- to fifty-year-olds, though some are older. They are not part of the front office, though admired lawyers who become section chiefs do not automatically lose their status as objects of admiration. They have more colorful personalities than the general run of their colleagues, they are more entertaining and personable in conversation, they are more gregarious and assertive, they have a higher opinion of themselves and a lower opinion of the policy makers in the front office. They have usually won one or more of the division's most important cases, whose names these lawyers then seem to carry attached to their own, like knighthoods won on the battlefield. Within the division, one might be referred for information not simply to "John Smith" but to "John Smith-he-tried-the-Universal-Widget-case."

Many of them arrived in the division before the significant increase in antitrust activity, and they express gratitude toward the older lawyers from whom they learned their trade. "I was advised to get some government experience," one of them explained his entry into the division:

Antitrust law wasn't the "in thing" it is now. It was a *very* esoteric field. It was just an accident that I got into it. I *thought* I was only going to be here for two years; that's how long I gave myself.

What I did when I first got here was to sit in the library for two weeks. Then I was introduced to . . . a superb lawyer, _____. I was assigned to work for *him*. I carried his briefcase for six or seven years, and I learned a fantastic amount. It was this—the personal relationships, and the quality of the men—that made me stay. And it was all so varied and fascinating—I'd no sooner get done with one thing than there'd be something else. My experience wasn't unusual. The people who came with me were lucky. . . . There was a whole corps of magnificent men to learn from. . . . But most of them are no longer here; they're out in private practice making money. Since then there's been the big boom in antitrust—we're valuable now. So anyone who's left around here has made a real sacrifice.

"Carrying someone's briefcase," one of them remarked of his apprenticeship,

can be debilitating—not to get into court. But if you're lucky, he'll use you—maybe to argue discovery motions. . . . But only if you've got something on the ball. You just can't risk *losing.* If you lose on one of these discovery motions, the case might take months longer—or you might not have a case at all. And I'm on the criminal side. Every mistake could throw you out of court. Something comes out of your mouth, and you know right away what you've said, and you look at the defense counsel, and you know right away what he's going to do. He asks the judge if he can approach the bench, and he says, "Your Honor, I move for a mistrial."

The appreticeship, then, is justified by the rigorous nature of courtroom combat.

Some of these lawyers have made their reputations mainly through the trial of structural rather than conduct cases. But even some of those who have tried important structural cases express a preference for "conduct" work:

The role of the division is to enforce the antitrust laws. But you don't have to make a choice between the clearest violations and the cases with the biggest effects; we have both behavior and structural cases. I've never thought about allocating resources between the two. But I'd always take a price-fixing case over a merger. . . . In a merger case, you work at your desk. There's no excitement.

Furthermore, they are, to say the least, not reluctant to talk about what they think of the front office when it attempts to alter their priorities. "I had one case," one of them remembered,

and it was a really nasty one—with the _____ industry on the _____ Coast. The subcontractors had competed, but then the primary contractors had hired house men to do the job and started compelling everyone to use them. The firms that had been cut out complained. Not the shippers, they were too small and too scared. I thought it would be a case—but it took these guys from Harvard across the street long enough to approve it. _____ kept telling me that it was too small for me, that I was too "valuable" to waste on things like that. But this was really *nasty.*

And more generally, another of these lawyers commented on division management:

You need a lawyer to run this place. . . . _____ [a recent assistant attorney general]? Don't *talk* to me about him. He wasn't a lawyer —he was an economics professor from _____, and he should have stayed there. . . . He came up with the "shared monopoly" idea. We looked at a bunch of things—but it was a bust. The trouble is that none of these industries actually *fit* the theory they had dreamed up. . . . I don't know whether shared monopoly is the only major new theory that ever came down from the top, but I think so. I wouldn't want to try a case on that theory—I think it stinks. You're trying to prove intent, but you have no *evidence*. They just react to each other—necessarily. The whole area is spooky. . . . It would be impossible to start developing cases from economic theories and data. . . . There's not enough money or personnel to find cases that way.

The style of such a lawyer, and the attitudes his colleagues seem to find admirable, are apparent enough from statements such as these. He is proud of having been trained to be an aggressive, bright but nonintellectual, technically competent, two-fisted prosecutor. He conceives of himself as an adversary, and he wants to win; but more than that, he wants to win by virtue of his character —his persuasiveness, hard work, canniness, and charm—as much as by force of his intellect. He conceives of his practice of law as an active and combative occupation rather than as a calling that at times resembles academic scholarship in the thoroughness of its research and its concern with clarity and distinctions. And antitrust law attracts him not because of its close connection with economic theory but because its cases are exciting cases, with important consequences and with powerful men for opponents. Forced to make the choice, he would rather have strong evidence than an elegant theory, and he expresses vocal resentment of anyone or any argument that would force him to reverse this order of concerns.

Their colleagues participate in but do not fully emulate these admired lawyers in the strength of such attitudes, and one important respect in which the "stars" differ from the other lawyers is in the intensity of their expressed resentment toward the organization's upper levels—the front office. One hears from all division lawyers the unsurprising complaints about the "bureaucracy," "too many lawyers," "too much red tape," and the fact that "things take too much time." But most lawyers, and especially the younger ones, seem to have no systematic quarrel with their superiors' authority. In fact, they profess at least a rhetorical sympathy with the need to have someone riding herd on individual lawyers. "I guess it has to be that way," was a comment whose substance was often repeated among them. "You have to have someone with a broader view of things; you can't have guys running around bringing whatever cases they want." The animus against the front office is wide-spread, but its verbal expressions tend to be mild.

The "star" lawyers, on the other hand, display no such restraint in speaking of their formal superiors. They have a greater personal investment in the division: they know they are prized by the organization or at least by important parts of it, they regard themselves as lawyers as good as or better than any of their superiors, and they display a mixture of outrage and contempt for anyone who presumes to pass judgment on their work. "What do they do?" one of these lawyers asked rhetorically, speaking of the people in the front office who review the staff lawyers' recommendations. "Have you ever seen a law review? Do you know what the editor does? He edits. They change. . . . They may be performing a great service—but I don't know; I try to have as little contact with them as possible." So becoming widely admired as a career lawyer in the division does not entail any special piety toward the organization as represented by its hierarchy. On the contrary, it is almost invariably accompanied by a readily articulated antihierarchical animus.

In sum, division lawyers show little inclination to take their models and attitudes directly from their observations of the organization's executive levels. Whether they see their long-term careers in the division or in the private antitrust bar, they see those careers as professional ones, not formed by the administrative or the political concerns of their nominal division superiors. Their reasons for being in the division and their future plans make them more inclined to learn from and emulate other staff lawyers. They are convinced of the broader social and economic worth of their work but do not take their bearings from any comprehensive or systematic social or economic philosophy apart from the most general, and not always very helpful, conviction that competition is a good thing. They lack the moral zealot's belief in the true turpitude of his adversaries. But their own statements reveal that the kind of zeal they do embrace is the zeal for prosecution, and their choice of colleagues whom they especially admire reveals something of what they think that impulse should entail. A good antitrust lawyer, to judge by these models, prosecutes aggressively wherever he can, and with pride in his technical craftsmanship. He procecutes *sine ira et studio;* he is aggressive but not moralistic. He is not willing to be deterred by theories of antitrust and its functions that could take a violation of the law out of his reach; instead, the test he applies to his opportunities for prosecution is the test of the criteria of the courtroom as he understands them.

In all of this one finds a surprising continuity over time: These are attitudes and interests that mirror to a considerable extent the ambiguities that many have seen in the Sherman Act itself and in the spirit of the organization Thurman Arnold refounded. Yet to say that a particular prosecutorial ethos pervades the division staff is by no means to explain how these lawyers, in the course of their work, make the particular decisions they do. It is all very well to say that the personal incentives of many division members and the attitudes that are presented to them as admirable combine to foster a general presumption in favor of prosecution wherever possible; it is another thing to describe what they consider a fit vehicle for prosecution. That description is the task of the next chapter.

4
Staff Decisions

Most information about possible antitrust violations comes to the division in one of the following ways.[1] The first source is complaints—from citizens, from businessmen (or their lawyers) with a personal interest in the practices complained of, from congressmen in behalf of constituents, and from other government agencies. The second source, one of minor importance in most areas,[2] is reports that business firms are compelled by law to file with government agencies such as the Securities and Exchange Commission. The third is the general and business press—including, for example, the *Wall Street Journal, Standard Corporation Reports,* and various trade publications. The fourth is personal contacts the division lawyers have with businessmen, fellow attorneys, and "civilian" friends. The fifth is studies occasionally undertaken concerning specific industries or practices.

The lawyers say that their superiors in the division make no attempt to withhold any of these categories of information from them. Some lawyers do worry that whole classes of potentially useful information never come to the division at all—cases of price-fixing in industries where "no one will squeal," violations that go unreported because they occur in industries that do not deal extensively with small businessmen who have both sufficient financial interest to complain and sufficient need to use government resources to redress their grievances, and mergers among small, privately held companies that may have considerable power in local markets. But there is little doubt among the lawyers that whatever useful information the division gets, some staff lawyer gets.

Furthermore, the lawyers say that they will almost always receive permission to open an investigation of an item that seems interesting to them and will usually be permitted to continue an investigation for as long as they think necessary.[3]

The lawyers believe they are their own bosses when it comes to recommendations about whether the results of an investigation warrant prosecution. This is not to say that they believe they have the final word in these decisions; on the contrary, they display a highly developed sensitivity to the ultimate sanctions wielded by the "front office"—that is, the assistant attorney general—and they exhibit a certain pride in what they consider their distance from the concerns of the hierarchy. Neither do the lawyers feel their independence to be the same thing as isolation from the judgments of peers and senior colleagues; on the contrary, the lawyers' judgments in these matters are informed by the opinions that prevail among staff lawyers and by the frequent conversations in which these opinions are expressed.

The staff lawyers' independence is one of the division's most important characteristics. Its basis is professional: the presence of a specific body of knowledge—in this case, of the antitrust laws as interpreted by the courts and of how to win cases in the courts—to which all members of the organization defer, no matter what their position in the hierarchy. Staff attorneys think that they have been trained well enough if not to be free of the necessity for further learning, then at least to have an authority for making judgments that is separate from and superior to the merely hierarchical authority of the division's executives.[4]

The lawyers' independence is reinforced by the institutional corollaries of legal professionalism: the division's almost exclusive dependence on the courts for the success of its cases and the presence in those courts of private antitrust lawyers who are not only professional colleagues but adversarial critics of the division's product. Antitrust cases being long and expensive to prepare,[5] there are sharp limits to the front office's willingness to supplant the staff's standards with other criteria when these latter are unacceptable to the courts, to the antitrust bar as a whole, and thus to the staff lawyers themselves.

One sign of this independence is that the lawyers defend their judgments on the basis of extensively articulated reasoning. The same independence allows them to think—and their superiors to acknowledge—that their interpretation of the division's proper course of action may be as compelling as that of their superiors. "We're supposed to be making professional judgments," one relatively new lawyer observed in a statement that sums up the prevailing attitude. "It's rare to be *ordered* to do anything. If I didn't think a case was any good, and the section chief thought it was, most likely he'd try to *persuade* me to keep on it. And if he couldn't, he'd have to find someone else. . . . No one could order me to recommend something I didn't *want* to recommend." As will be described later, there are in fact informal ways of persuading the staff lawyers to change their formal decisions and recommendations. But the possibility of such persuasion in no way contradicts— indeed, the necessity for persuasion may be taken as evidence of—the lawyers' determination to make their own judgments. The attorneys act as professionals, and the organization takes account of this fact.

Constraints on Prosecution: Information

Formally, the staff lawyers make three major sets of decisions when they receive an item of information: whether to begin a preliminary investigation, whether to ask for a full investigation, and whether to recommend prosecution. It is tempting to consider each of these decisions in turn, but such treatment would impose a spurious order on the lawyers' work. According to the division's organization manual, for instance, a staff lawyer cannot spend more than five working days on a preliminary investigation without receiving formal permission from his section chief to change his inquiry to "full investigation" status. In practice, this distinction seems to make very little impression on the lawyers. Several of them had to refer to their own copies of the manual in order to describe what the distinction was, and several of them mentioned prosecutions of their own that emerged from work that had never formally received, as far as they could remember, the title of "full investigation." Thus the lawyers' reasons for beginning or terminating a preliminary investigation are not essentially different from their reasoning about a full investigation or even a final recommendation; a lawyer may conduct a full investigation but recommend against prosecution because of information that, had he had it earlier, would have stopped the investigation at the preliminary stage.

The formal categories do not seem to have much effect on how the lawyers deal with information that comes to them. Instead, they see their information in simpler categories, according to whether it is useful for purposes of prosecution or not. And most of it is not.

An interviewer who suggests to a staff lawyer that he exercises discretion in the choice of division prosecutions will almost invariably be met with some impolite expression of disbelief. Staff lawyers do not feel that they have very much latitude in the decisions they make, especially with regard to their initial decisions on whether or not to investigate an incoming piece of information. While this reaction cannot be taken as the last word on the question of their latitude, their reasons for the disclaimer and the constraints they feel are crucial to understanding how they use the discretion they do in fact possess.

Staff lawyers have little discretion, the vast majority of them explain, not because their superiors impose any special constraints on them but because so little of the information they receive is useful for purposes of prosecution. They know that some violations are grossly underreported to the division. But of the information the lawyers do receive, they see most as totally useless for their job, which is the job of building a case.

The first category of "useless information" that the lawyers mention includes almost all the complaints the division receives concerning "conduct" violations—illegal anticompetitive practices that do not directly affect the structure of ownership or control in an industry. What the lawyers are looking for when they search for a conduct violation can be fully described only by describing the antitrust case law. But the staff lawyers themselves simplify the case law in their minds for purposes of routine investigative work, and a much more radical simplification may give a rough idea of what the staff considers suitable material for prosecution.[6]

Under the antitrust laws, direct agreements among firms to fix the price of a commodity are in almost all cases illegal, no matter what the level at which the price is fixed and no matter what the economic situation the price-fixing was designed to remedy. Direct agreements to limit output are similarly illegal.

Also illegal are collective agreements among firms at different levels of a market under which supplies, orders, or preferential terms of sale or purchase are confined to an exclusive firm or group of firms. This prohibition includes a prohibition against "reciprocity," a kind of exclusive-dealing agreement in which both parties give favored treatment to each other.

"Bottleneck" agreements—under which those who control a scarce facility refuse to grant use of it to all competitors on a fair basis—are illegal.

Collective agreements to allocate market shares—by percentages, geographic classes of customers, particular transactions, end uses of products, or the like—are almost always illegal.

Monopolization of a market, or the attempt to monopolize it, or conspiracy to monopolize it, is illegal. If a firm has achieved a "dominant position" in a market and decides on its own to engage in any of the forbidden anticompetitive practices, even without any collusion with other firms, it may be guilty of an attempt to monopolize.

Any reader of even this highly abbreviated list will see immediately how many borderline questions of fact and theory are thrown up by such bald formulations. To name only one of the most important, proof of all these violations, except for some cases of monopolization or attempts to monopolize, requires showing that there was in fact some agreement among the conspirators, that some "meeting of the minds" occurred. Even in the case of unilateral monopolization, one must in theory present at least some attenuated evidence of intent. In some cases, a "meeting of the minds," or intent, can be inferred directly from the existence of an agreement or from effects that could not possibly have occurred without some such agreement or intent; but in most cases, the evidence is considerably less clear.

As they look over the information they receive, the staff attorneys are almost never concerned with such difficulties; for almost none of the "conduct" complaints the lawyers receive seem to them to provide even the beginnings of a case. To begin with, the lawyers receive a significant amount of what they call "simple crackpot mail." "I get letters from this guy in California," one lawyer gave an example, "talking about how the _____ industry is just one big Jewish conspiracy. . . . "

The lawyers must also answer complaints about alleged conduct that, even if it has occurred, simply does not constitute an antitrust violation. In this category fall most letters from consumers who complain about an individual businessman's failure to provide satisfactory service. A lawyer will usually answer this type of letter by referring the complainant to another, more appropriate government agency, by sending the letter himself directly to the proper agency, or by requesting additional information that might provide evidence of an antitrust violation. The complaining party rarely answers a request of this kind.

Even when the complainant does allege a proper antitrust violation—say, price-fixing, a boycott, or predatory price-cutting—he usually does not answer if a division lawyer writes back to ask him for more specific information. Most letters of this type allege a violation of law—they note a price rise, for instance, and conclude that "the _____ industry *must* be fixing prices," one lawyer read from a complaint—but they give no actual evidence that any violation has occurred. "We write back for more information," another attorney summarized the procedure in these cases, "and 90 percent of the time they never write back."

If a complainant does write back, supplying particulars of an alleged violation, he may turn out upon brief examination to have been misleading the division—deliberately or not—about these particulars. A lawyer gave one example of how his time was, as he said, "wasted" in this way:

I had a recent thing—a guy from _____. He was a _____ distributor, and he said the company had cut him off because he'd started carrying someone else's products. . . . But those facts just weren't *there*. There were sixty distributors in the same situation, but only three had been cut off—and those three were for good business reasons. It was always a question of the facts; and this guy was just using us.

In itself that fact that the division is being "used" for private gain by no means antagonizes the lawyers; they realize that most of the information they receive will come from self-interested complaints. "If it *had* been a violation," this lawyer continued, "we would have gone forward anyway."[7] But the self-interest of complainants does build a systematic unreliability into the information and so contributes to the large number of "useless" complaints the division receives.

Two different points can be made about the four kinds of complaints that elicit only pro forma action by the lawyers. For one thing, the insubstantiality of the complaints and the large amount of time they consume make the lawyers think that they do not exercise much discretion in choosing cases for prosecution. They do not see themselves working in an environment of plentiful prosecution opportunities among which discretionary choices must be made. Instead, they see their environment as marked by a scarcity of such information.

Second, though, the lawyers feel this "scarcity" partly as a result of the way they conceive of their proper task. They do not consider themselves comprehensive economy regulators, ready to seize upon any pretext for investigating the practices and structure of a given industry. If they did, they might see these vague, irresponsible, or undocumented complaints as opportunities for more systematic investigation rather than merely as sources of fruitless and frustrating "busywork." But they do not.

This does not mean that the lawyers habitually hew to the narrowest possible conception of their role. Indeed, as it will be argued later, they often are ingenious about finding new violations when the orginally suspected wrongdoing does not materialize. Nevertheless, for a complaint to be "useful" in their minds, it must provide not only a hypothesis about where a violation might be occurring or where there might be some dysfunction in the economy but at least the beginnings of evidence admissible in court. It must give some presumption that it can become a case. Information that provides such a presumption is almost always investigated. Furthermore, if its promise materializes, it will be recommended for prosecution—on the basis of whether the case can be won rather than according to more arcane criteria such as that of the most efficient use of Antitrust resources in the economy. "I have a price-fix now in _____," one young lawyer said. "I know it's too small to bother with. But *I* found it, and sure, I'll recommend it."

Another type of complaint that is investigated but quickly disposed of involves an offense with the following characteristics: It is small and isolated, it clearly involves no practice that is criminal, and it ceases as soon as the division informs the alleged violator that he is being investigated. "We got a complaint from a retail store that said _____ wouldn't sell to them. We wrote back to _____, but by the time they wrote back to us, they said they *were* selling to this guy. And when we wrote the retail store again to check, they confirmed it." Another lawyer told of a case he had recently closed dealing with the distribution of trading stamps. A local professional association had ruled that all of its members were to discontinue using the stamps in their independently owned retail stores. Almost as soon as the division began investigating a complaint it had received about this practice, the association rescinded its ban. It was clear to the investigating lawyer that an antitrust violation had occurred. "But," as he told the story, "it wasn't a clearly criminal boycott. And besides, what more good could we do? The association had already stopped the practice."

A similar reason for terminating an investigation quickly with a recommendation not to prosecute came from a lawyer who had received a complaint about an association that governed a relatively small professional sport. It was clear to the lawyer that the association was enforcing an illegal rule, but when he made contact with them, he said, "they changed it. It doesn't do any good to prosecute a past violation like that; you only get an injunction anyway."

These examples might seem to be exceptions to the generalization that the lawyers throw out only what will almost certainly not become a case; they therefore seem to belie the lawyers' contention that they have little opportunity to choose from among those situations that could probably be turned into legal victories. But not too much should be made of these exceptions. The cases all involved a very small amount of commerce, according to the lawyers' reckoning, and noncriminal practices that had been quickly abandoned with no continuing effects and that therefore offered little prospect of any additional relief being gained from a suit. No one of these characteristics would by itself be a bar to prosecution in most of the lawyers' minds; it seems to require a combination of all three, or at least one of them in extremis, to discourage the staff lawyer from taking the investigation seriously as a possible prosecution.

In light of this perceived scarcity of information, one might suppose that where minor complaints come from might make a difference in the lawyers' treatment of them. One might suppose, for instance, that there would be no bar to giving specially close attention to complaints sponsored by the politically powerful. But this does not seem to be the case. There seem to be very few individual "conduct violation" complaints sponsored by the White House. There are more from congressmen writing in behalf of their constituents. In one respect, congressional mail is treated differently from other complaints: By front office directive, all congressional mail must be answered within forty-eight hours. But though the mail is answered quickly, the actual investigation need not be conducted with any special speed or according to any special standards. It is *after* he answers a congressman's letter that a lawyer must go about deciding what the information in it is worth to him. And at this second stage, there is simply no evidence that the congressional complaints receive special treatment. The lawyers say they are as likely to throw them out as they are to discard any other complaint. Certainly there is no formal directive to give them special consideration, and the staff reports no informal pressures, either. One lawyer gave a typical summary of the staff attitude: "Congressional mail? I treat it just like anything else. The politics doesn't mean a thing to me." As will be discussed later, Congress has other opportunities to influence the division's conduct but these do not seem to extend to the establishment of separate criteria by which the staff lawyers consider congressionally sponsored complaints.

"Conduct" complaints are not the only kind of information that the lawyers don't think generally promising. News of "structural" violations as well (situations or courses of action that affect the pattern of ownership or control in an industry)[8] is also mostly what the lawyers call "a waste of time." This second type of information comes chiefly from the business and financial press, from companies resisting take-overs, or from companies that seek the division's opinion on the legality of a prospective merger. When the division receives such information, the section chiefs assign it to one or more lawyers for inspection, just as they do in the case of information about conduct. Before he assigns these items, a section chief has already made his own assessment of an item's probable worth; so, while an experienced lawyer may sometimes receive a clipping that "doesn't look like anything" to the section chief if the lawyer has special knowledge of the industry involved, it is usually the younger lawyers who get the low-potential information.

As with the conduct complaints, what the lawyer is looking for in these pieces of news must be described by describing the state of the case law—and the state of this kind of case law is even more difficult to characterize than is the law on conduct violations. Generally, the lawyers are looking for evidence that the merger or joint

venture at hand may, in the words of the Clayton Act, "substantially . . . lessen competition, or . . . tend to create a monopoly."
The lawyers look for the following first indications that such may
be the case: Two firms are in direct competition in some significant
degree; or the degree of competition is not so significant, but the
market is already highly concentrated or displays a "trend" toward
increased concentration; or the merger entails the disappearance
of a competitor who is not now a significant factor in a market
but who possesses some special asset that could make him one
someday.

In the case of "vertical" mergers—purchases by firms of their
suppliers or customers—a lawyer will try to determine the extent
to which access to the newly merged firms is "foreclosed" to other
competitors. With both "vertical" mergers and "horizontal" ones
(in which the merging firms produce the same commodity), the
lawyer will ask his questions not only of firms actually in a given
market but also of "potential" entrants into the market. In the case
of a merger with no clear "vertical" or "horizontal" aspects, the
lawyer will nevertheless look for some way in which the merger
might be construed as anticompetitive: With "conglomerate"
mergers, he will ask in particular whether the merger will foreclose
sections of various markets by establishing new opportunities for
the practice of reciprocity or whether a merger is liable to "entrench" an already powerful firm by providing it with a new influx of products, markets, resources, connections, or preferential
terms of trade.

This description, like the brief description of "conduct" violations, raises immediate questions: At what level can these practices be said to have a "substantial" effect, as specified by law?
How are relevant markets to be defined? How much are probable
effects to be judged on the basis of "objective" information about
the firms' characteristics and how much on the basis of past records of conduct and statements of intention?

The lawyers who receive merger information rarely feel that they
must ask such questions in any detail. When he receives such information, a staff lawyer will first gather from standard library
sources basic information about the size of the companies involved, their products, and their financial condition. He may also

refer to trade publications for information about company histories and industry structure and trends. He may look up past division cases and investigations involving the companies or the industry, or he may consult other division lawyers with experience in the area. On the basis of these sources, he will decide whether to write to the merging companies for more information—in other words, to take the first step toward making his investigation more than cursory.

One lawyer described the usual outcome of these preliminary searches: "Ninety percent of these things are bummers." The lawyers report three major reasons why most of these investigations do not progress beyond the most preliminary stage. By far the most important is size. The acquisition of a company whose annual sales are one million dollars is described by most lawyers as "nothing," one hundred million dollars is "big," and in between the two extremes, five to ten million dollars dollars, is the amount they usually report that they will "take a second look at." Most of the lawyers say that there is no absolute minimum on the size of an acquisition that will appear "interesting" to them; they say only that the bigger the acquisition and the acquiring company, the more likely they are to "look very closely."

With most small mergers, a second factor in the lawyers' decisions is the presence or absence of evidence that any special factor—the possible monopolization of an important technological innovation, for instance, or foreclosure of a small but somehow crucial market—might reverse the presumption against devoting more time to the situation. When such a factor appears, a lawyer will almost certainly seek more information; when he does not, it is because he cannot see any special twist.

The third major reason for the early termination of a merger investigation, or a final negative recommendation on prosecution, is that even a large merger or joint venture—in terms of both absolute size and market shares—may turn out simply not to be anticompetitive. One of the companies may clearly fall under the "failing company" doctrine: It is on the verge of permanent failure; it has tried and failed to find an outside, independent purchaser; and industry conditions as a whole are such as to discourage the appearance of one. The lawyers do not make this judgment lightly; it seems to occur among them chiefly where the product involved is clearly obsolescent or when the lawyer has become convinced of the industry's troubles through recent past investigations he has made. Thus one lawyer remembered that he had "approved" a merger between two companies whose common product had been made obsolescent by modern shipping methods. And even apart from truly "failing" companies, economic conditions may determine whether a practice is anticompetitive or not. To demonstrate this, one lawyer displayed a *Wall Street Journal* clipping announcing a joint venture by two large companies that were direct competitors; it had been sent to him because of his familiarity with the industry. "Looks good, doesn't it? But it's not. I know that industry. It's in lousy shape. Neither of these companies could do this alone."

The importance in attorneys' minds of these reasons for inaction—for not investigating a merger, for dropping the investigation quickly, or for recommending against prosecution—should not be exaggerated. The absolute size of the acquiring and acquired companies and the degree of concentration in an industry are certainly the factors of greatest interest to the lawyers. But size and concentration are not the only factors—and certainly size and concentration alone do not stop the division from considering certain cases. The division has brought cases against relatively small firms and in industries of low concentration. And the lawyers profess themselves quite willing to continue to do so if they can find in a merger some special argument, drawn from the whole range of past and possible future court decisions, that might brand a merger as anticompetitive. In the same spirit, they are not prone to believe a company that claims financial hardship and argues that its merger is therefore not really anticompetitive. They say that such a claim is no bar to prosecution unless a lawyer can convince himself that there is truly compelling evidence to support it, and convince himself against a strong presumption to the contrary. It is true that the lawyers may sometimes overlook a possible argument that can be used against a merger, but when this happens, it must usually be judged a failure of imagination rather than of will. If 90 percent of the merger notices they receive are "bummers," it is because the lawyers themselves see them to be unambiguously lawful under the antitrust statutes.

Somewhere between 80 and 90 percent of the matters that come across an Antitrust lawyer's desk are, according to those interviewed, given no more than a few days' investigating time, and even of those matters to which the lawyers say they have devoted more than a minimal amount of time, fewer than half are recommended for prosecution.[9] As far as one can tell from these interviews, three reasons account for the vast majority of all these negative decisions. Either something is by no stretch of the imagination an antitrust violation, or the lawyer sees no hope of finding evidence to prove it in court, or there is no possible relief to be gained from prosecution. Decisions made for these reasons, in most cases, are highly consensual; they are agreed upon by the lawyer making the decision, by his colleagues, and by superiors. The lawyer does not think he is exercising any discretion in turning down such cases; he turns them down because he sees no chance of making or winning them. He is almost never exercising any purely personal preference for "going easy" on any particular industry or type of violation, whether from some competing theoretical considerations or for more idiosyncratic reasons. He builds his cases where he can; the chief constraint he feels is the scarcity of information from which to construct them.

Finding a Case

This picture of the lawyers' operating procedures argues that the lawyers are particularistic in their decisions, judging each piece of information according to whether it contributes to a successful prosecution; that most of the work is a process of turning down cases for prosecution; and that one could hardly do better in describing the reasons for these rejections than to describe antitrust case law, federal rules of evidence, and the facts available in the particular case at hand.

This picture is, however, incomplete. First of all, it suggests a subservience to "the law" in its current state that contradicts our previous picture of the staff attorney as an aggressive prosecutor, trying to maximize his prosecutorial reach. But more important, it ignores two obvious facts. The first is that in many areas the antitrust law is ambiguous. Even where the law as interpreted by the courts clearly prohibits certain categories of conduct, it may not be clear whether the conduct at hand falls into the proscribed category. Or there may be a special exemption for the group in question that makes it unclear whether the law can be applied.[10] And sometimes the law is in dispute with regard to even more fundamental questions.

Moreover, the interpretation of the antitrust laws has changed in major ways since their passage—and many of these changes have occurred as a direct result of new arguments that the division has made before the courts. It is not merely that staff lawyers value aggressive prosecution; it is that they actually behave as aggressive prosecutors, in ways that significantly affect antitrust doctrine. Staff lawyers explicitly claim that most changes in antitrust laws emerged from the minds of government trial attorneys. "Every new idea around here," as one of them put it, "has been discussed up and down these corridors for years."

So if most staff lawyers spend the bulk of their time discarding matters they see as unambiguously beyond the reach of the antitrust laws and of the division, this does not mean that they consider themselves absolutely bound by the law as it stands. On the contrary, part of the division's prevailing definition of a good prosecutor entails precisely the ability to bring into prosecutorial reach situations that on first inspection would seem to be beyond that reach. And this definition has consequences for the way the staff deals with situations that are ambiguous.

One factor in particular is crucial to understanding how the lawyers treat a doubtful situation—the length and complexity of antitrust investigations. The length of these investigations, if they are not very quickly disposed of, is commonly measured not in weeks but in months or years. One lawyer noted that his section chief did not even begin to ask seriously how an investigation was going until four months after it had begun. Another staffer complained that these investigations took much too long; more of them, he said, could be done quickly and still be done well, as had happened on an important case of his in which special time pressures had forced the division to move with unusual speed. When asked how long this "quick" investigation had gone on, he answered, "Ten months."

The reason for this extreme length is a matter of dispute. Some lawyers claim that the division itself, both front office and staff, is simply slower than it need be, particularly when a case is not especially exciting or when there is no special need—such as that provided by the pending consummation of a merger—to move quickly. One young lawyer told how, when he had first arrived in the division, "We worked all the time on the _____ case. I didn't even go home for Thanksgiving. I loved it. But I wouldn't do that for any of the cases I'm working on now." But it is also pointed out that when the division does have some special reason to move quickly—for instance, when it does want to stop a merger from being consummated so that it can avoid the problems posed by divestiture—it can prepare its motions for preliminary injunctions with some speed.

There is another probable reason for the extreme length. When dealing with "structural" violations, the division lawyers claim that they would be perfectly happy to bring cases on the basis of less evidence than they currently present, with more exclusive reliance on what they call "objective" economic data and less attention to company history, practices, and motives. But, they say, federal judges would simply not be persuaded by such "bare bones" arguments. The judges are not social scientists, the lawyers observe; even when dealing with a statute such as the Clayton Act, which does not require the presence of any anticompetitive motives in order for the court to bar a company's action, the courts persist in seeking out such motives, or their absence, in a wealth of detail concerning the particular firms at issue.

It is not clear how much credence should be given to this explanation. Other staff lawyers discount their colleagues' opinion that the courts contribute to the length of investigations. District court judges, they think, would be only too happy to have shorter antitrust briefs and trials to deal with. The staff lawyers, they say, fill their briefs, arguments, and investigative time with a wealth of detail because *they* are not persuaded by exclusively economic arguments, even where these might be thought to suffice.

Still other lawyers point to an additional reason for the length of investigations. Defense counsel, they say, often obstruct the division's efforts to gather information. The staff admits that defense counsel tend to delay partly because they know that there is often no particular time pressure on the division lawyers, but the staff also claims that their opponents' major motive is simply their interest in extending the time available for merger plans to be completed, for the facts of a general situation to change, or for prosecution witnesses to grow dim in their recollection of past events. Some members of the private antitrust bar said that this was true, at least in the case of mergers. One of them explained that he was happy to see his current merger litigation with the division go on as long as possible: "These things are harder to break up once the eggs are scrambled." And another ex–defense attorney joked about his past career, "Ah, yes, I remember the room where we let the government lawyers examine our documents—the one with the cigar smoke piped in." A division lawyer pointed out that in the field of banking, where a special statute automatically bars any merger beginning at the time the division announces its intention to challenge it until the case is concluded, the gathering of facts proceeds much more quickly and without so much delay by the defense.

The division keeps no statistics on the length of its investigations. But a rough estimate from these interviews is that in even the relatively quick banking investigations, the usual duration is six months or more. So one must conclude that important reasons for this length lie in the nature of the investigative process itself and in the lawyers' expectations of these investigations.

In the first place, making most antitrust cases simply requires large amounts of information, much of which is difficult to collect, digest, and interpret. Monopolization cases provide the most extreme example. Division lawyers must have, in effect, a complete history of the firm under investigation—its organization, its practices and pricing policies, its internal growth and acquisitions, its relations with customers, competitors, and suppliers, its record of patents and of research and innovation in general—as well as information on industry structure, technical knowledge of the firm's products, and histories of the firm's competitors. One such recently active investigation file, lawyers report, contained well over one hundred thousand documents, outside of information from publications and from interviews conducted by the lawyers themselves or by the FBI. Indeed, older lawyers in the division are convinced that one reason the division did not make more effort until recently to affect industry structure through monopolization prosecutions is that their younger colleagues, eager to expand their experience by participating in a series of cases and proceedings, were not so eager to undertake investigations of the length that a monopolization case requires.

Even a "simple" merger case may entail, as did a recent investigation that one lawyer described, an examination of over fifty thousand documents, and criminal price-fixing cases may also require a detailed examination of industry structure and history and of pricing patterns. Obviously, the lawyers develop special skill and judgment in deciding which documents and pieces of information merit careful scrutiny. Still, the lawyers uniformly and persuasively point out that the work is inherently time-consuming and filled with drudgery. As one much-respected division lawyer said, "Ninety-five percent of my work is just digging up those facts."

As a result of the large amount of time required to develop anything that has substantial promise of becoming a case, the staff lawyers have considerable personal interest in seeing the matter grow into a prosecution. And because the work involved means that not very many case possibilities will be open to a lawyer at one time, the attorneys want to see to it that what they work on for so long finally bears fruit.

The lawyers themselves certainly say that this is true. "Once you've spent so much time on one of these damn things," one of them remarked, "you tend to get pretty attached to it." And to a surprisingly large extent, the staff feels supported in this attitude by the section chiefs and even the front office. This is not to say that the higher levels of the organization are no more critical of the lawyers' work than the lawyers themselves are. But the section chiefs, as well as the lawyers directly involved, are reluctant to close a substantial investigation. The prevailing attitude was expressed in virtually the same words by both a staff lawyer and a section chief: "If something goes on long enough," the lawyer said, "you *know* there's got to be something there." And his section chief said, "If you press hard enough, *something* will come out." A frequently heard comment among the staff lawyers was the observation that "it's twice as hard to get permission to close an investigation around here as it is to open one." So not only does the length of the investigation dispose the lawyers to continue each one until some case emerges, there also seems to be a lack of pressure from superiors to counter this disposition.

This impulse to find a case where one has investigated expresses itself in several ways. In the first place, the staff lawyers are over-whelmingly likely to resolve their own doubts about the worth and probable success of a case in favor of prosecution. This point will be discussed more extensively later on; here it need only be said that in at least 80 percent of the cases that the lawyers themselves mentioned as being "hard" for them to decide about, they finally recommended that the division prosecute. One lawyer in the section that handles banking matters, a field especially plagued with problems of theory and evidence, was asked about the cases in which he had recommended against prosecution. He answered, "I can't think of a case where the staff *didn't* want to sue. . . . If we don't act, it's because we have absolutely no cause."

The second way this impulse to prosecute is expressed is in the lawyers' attempts to extend the reach of the antitrust laws. These attempts occur, with slight variations, both in the cases where the lawyers feel the state of the law to be fairly clear on what consti-tutes a prohibited action and in those cases where the law is not so clear.

When they are dealing with types of offenses already clearly pro-hibited, the lawyers tend to exercise their ingenuity on matters of proof and jurisdiction. They admit freely that even when they are fairly sure of the offense they are going to allege and the arguments by which they are going to try to prove it, they examine much more factual material than is likely to be directly relevant. They simply do not want to stop sifting through their material until they have culled every piece of evidence for their argument. Even if they al-ready think they have a strong case, they want it to be stronger. "We're all looking," one lawyer laughed, "for the magic document in the last box." Thus their desire to make a case out of each investigation is not only an effect of the long investigations but a cause of them as well.

Just as important, the lawyers take some pride in their ability to solve practical problems of evidence in new ways. Some of these discoveries involve ingenious proofs. During grand jury proceedings concerning an alleged price-fixing, one attorney had been temporarily frustrated by the defendant companies' claims that their prices *appeared* to change simultaneously, but in fact did so only because each company, in preparing its catalogs and price lists, responded to price changes revealed in its rivals' most recent new catalogs. "But I looked at those catalogs," the lawyer remembered, "and I noticed that they were very thick. I figured it must take quite a while to print them. So I checked with the printing companies, and I found out that the last printing order had come in *before* the first catalog had come out."

The lawyers also try to extend their reach by applying existing antitrust law to lines of commerce or geographical areas where it has never been applied before. One attorney claimed as noteworthy a relatively small and clear case that had been brought in an American protectorate where the antitrust law had never been previously applied.

Another staff attorney described as novel a case in which the "new" feature was the line of commerce. It involved a regulated industry that because of economic and technical requirements held a series of legal local monopolies over the service it provided. The industry practice was to agree to supply this service only to privately owned distributors, while refusing to deal with distributors owned by municipalities. The lawyer described his argument: "The _____ companies say they don't have to provide this service to the municipalities. But we say they're a bottleneck. . . . Yes, I suppose that *is* just a replay of the old AP [Associated Press] case. But it's a different thing to apply it, to prove it in *this* area."

Finally, the lawyers often have to solve new jurisdictional problems in order to extend substantively clear antitrust law into new lines of commerce. The lawyer quoted above went on to give one of the reasons why his case represented an advance for the reach of the antitrust laws and the reach of the division. "Unlike the AP case,"[11] he explained, "we have to deal with some new jurisdictional problems. We have to prove that the _____ [agency] doesn't have primary jurisdiction over this particular practice."

In cases such as these, where the law is relatively clear, two further tendencies may be seen in the staff lawyers' exercise of their inventive energies. The first is related to the structure of available opportunity. At present, the regulated industries present the largest lines of commerce previously untapped by the division and thus the greatest opportunities for new prosecutions under established antitrust principles. So many of the problems that the lawyers mention as new and exciting deal with attempts to reach a certain line of regulated commerce by limiting the jurisdiction that its regulatory agency can exercise.

Second, several lawyers mentioned that certain types of offenses, offenses they found especially heinous, would move them to make particularly vigorous efforts at investigation and argument. Most of these lawyers said they held a special animus against boycotts; if a pattern of action even vaguely suggested one, they would try very hard to prove that it *was* one. And one lawyer, somewhat more idiosyncratically, began his own list of odious offenses by saying, "Tie-ins. I'll always 'reach' on a tie-in."

So far, these examples of innovation on the lawyers' part seem relatively trivial. The law is clear; the question is one of proof or jurisdiction; the invention that takes place is of a relatively low order; aside from a special attention to particularly predatory offenses, these exercises in ingenuity are ad hoc, determined largely by accidental difficulty or opportunity. The lawyers are perfectly aware of this. The reason, they say, is that in the area where inventions of this type occur, in the area of "conduct" violations, they are fairly well satisfied with the current state of the law. "Sure, there are always things to be done," one of them remarked, "patents, for instance. But with most of these violations, we already have good case law. Now you take merger law—*that's* where the action is."

It is undoubtedly merger law where the division lawyers think "the action is" and where individual lawyers think themselves the most theoretically creative. It has already been suggested that lawyers begin with a "list" of possible anticompetitive effects when they study a merger, that they will refuse to investigate a merger seriously only where it is very clear that none of them exist, and that they usually recommend against prosecution only where they have managed to find none. The converse, though, is also true: They will investigate wherever there is even the possibility of some anticompetitive effect. And it is not surprising that once such an investigation has begun, they will be reluctant to end it without "finding something there."

Therefore the first effect of the desire to find a merger case—as with conduct cases—is to lengthen investigations. The investigations in merger cases lengthen because, as the lawyers themselves say, they look for more kinds of anticompetitive effects than they can possibly hope to find. They begin investigations with a "feeling," as some of them say, that a particular merger is "a bad merger." This feeling (the attorneys tend to speak of it as ineffable intuition, the fruit of years of experience, as against mere calculation of probabilities) may amount to nothing more than a discovery of the obvious, as when a clearly illegal feature is almost certain to be present in a merger. One lawyer explained, talking about his decision to pursue a certain transportation merger, "[Company X] ran from [Point A] to [Point B], but they didn't carry any traffic from [Point B] to [Point C]. But if they bought [Company Y], which already has a lot of the [Point B–Point C] traffic, it was obvious that there was likely to be a foreclosure problem."

On the other hand, this "feeling" that a merger is "bad" may not have such obvious justification; indeed, it may have very little to do with the antitrust laws at all. One lawyer spoke of a merger that had on its face seemed relatively uninteresting:

They don't really compete directly; all their products are patented, anyway. But both these firms are now doing research in the _____ area, which I consider crucial to the future of mankind, and if they merge their research facilities, that development is going to slow down. I figured that's where the case was going to be.

Another lawyer told about a series of mergers between American companies in an industry and their counterparts in a foreign country, mergers that had come to his attention through public sources: "They looked okay. But what worried me about them was what if _____, _____, and _____ start using these foreign companies to produce all their component parts and take jobs away from American labor? The problem is that I don't know how to get *at* these things; I haven't found an argument to use." This particular lawyer evidently did manage to find an argument; a month after this statement, he was busily at work on an investigation to provide evidence for it.

So in these cases, investigation begins on the basis of suspicions rather than full-fledged theory. Sometimes the suspicion is only indirectly based on antitrust offenses per se; in that case, a lawyer must investigate various possibilities until he finds evidence that *does* bear on some category of antitrust violation. But even where a lawyer has an initial hypothesis about what is legally or economically wrong with a merger, he will not stop investigating if his search fails to bear out his original theory.

Thus investigations lengthen as lawyers try out a whole series of theories on a particular merger. Several lawyers talked about this process. One attorney spoke of mergers in the international field:

I'll look for direct competition first, of course—though there won't be any. I could try potential competition—but I suspect that's going to be a little hard, since there are *lots* of potential competitors of that type. I don't know. Maybe I can show that the companies were competitors in *other* parts of the world and could start allocating markets there to increase their profits. . . .

The last strategy he mentioned entailed a considerable increase in the information he would require.

Another young attorney told of a bank merger case in which the original staff inclination had been to challenge the merger exclusively on the theory that it removed an important potential independent competitor from the market. "But then," he remembered,

it appeared that there might be vertical foreclosure, too. It dealt with correspondent banking services that the [big city] banks perform for smaller ones. The small banks "pay" for this by keeping more money on deposit with the [big] banks than they need to. So we investigated the excess deposits—they're kept in a separate account—as a proxy measure of this business in correspondent services. Unfortunately, we only came up with a 1 percent foreclosure. . . .

Not only will the lawyers try out a whole series of arguments on a particular merger, they are not put off if the arguments seem at first glance to be internally inconsistent. This is not to say that they are always unable to reconcile these inconsistencies, but they are hardly what one would call fully self-critical in their deliberations. One lawyer was asked about seeming inconsistencies in the argument he was using in a certain case and about whether these presented an intellectual problem for him. "Intellectual problems?" he answered. "I may have trouble working this out, but I don't have any *intellectual* problems. A lot of this is mostly personal competitiveness. . . . " This was an advocate speaking, not a judge.

Attorneys gave other examples of how, during the course of investigations, they brought seemingly incompatible arguments "into line." One lawyer was describing a vertical merger he had investigated, in which a producer had bought one of the several firms that were supplying it with a particular component:

When we started, the foreclosure argument was very strong: We thought that _____ was foreclosed as a purchaser of _____, thus making it harder for anyone else to enter the supplier's business. But then it appeared that the customer itself might be a potential independent competitor in the supplier's business. Of course the potential competition argument isn't so strong, and it's still unclear. And there was a bigger problem: The arguments cut across each other. How can a company be both a potential purchaser and a potential independent competitor? But we did figure out a way to do both.

Another example of the same process occurred when an attorney was investigating a merger that appeared not to be anticompetitive—and appeared so because, according to the market definition the division was already using in another ongoing case, this staff lawyer's two companies were simply not in the same line of commerce: "So I started looking at both lines of commerce, to see if they could really be one line. . . . Of course defense counsel in both cases were communicating with each other and accusing us of using inconsistent theories. But . . . [we] worked it out." So the desire to make a case from each investigation leads to a very marked determination to "work out" theoretical inconsistencies.

But the same impulse, the impulse to find a merger case, has yet a third important effect: It encourages lawyers to improvise, to innovate, and to extend the law. Whether all these innovations are what an outsider would call substantial, and whether they represent sufficient progress in the direction that some observers want the antitrust laws to take, is quite another matter, though one on which the examples below may shed some light. But many of the attorneys who had worked on merger investigations could point to what they thought were genuinely new arguments developed in the course of their work.

It may be remembered, for instance, that a lawyer quoted above had argued that there could be "sublines" of commerce within a single line. The invention and acceptance of this argument were important, he said, because they increased the number of mergers the division could prosecute in related lines of commerce.

Another attorney said that he had invented a whole new category of anticompetitive effects under similar circumstances. He was convinced that a certain merger in a regulated industry was anticompetitive, and the division intervened in the regulatory agency proceeding that was to judge the merger. The lawyer's problem was that the two companies in question did not compete directly and could not be assumed to be capable of doing so in the foreseeable future. His response was a new argument to the agency about the circumstances under which companies could be said to be competing: "We're saying that even if they're in *different* territories they're competitive because they compete to have industries locate in their areas. And even newer than that, we're saying that there's 'yardstick competition'—different prices in *another* area can raise a public stink. . . . "

Even more extreme was the recounting by another lawyer who had responded to a particular problem of his by proposing—albeit unsuccessfully—a major reinterpretation of the Sherman Act. The lawyer's problem was a merger between two large firms, but in a market of such large absolute size (and without any significant trend toward concentration) that "substantially lessened competition" under the Clayton Act would be extremely difficult to argue. He found the answer to his problem, he reported, by rereading the first "trust-busting" cases brought under the Sherman Act. The law, as he read it, could apply to single mergers in a manner much broader than had been generally assumed since the passage of the

Clayton Act. And by attacking the merger under the Sherman Act, he said, he would be free of the necessity to deal with the merging firms' relatively small market shares.

Thus an important effect of the lawyers' desire to make cases is a certain tendency to try to stretch the law to cover what it did not quite fit before. As with "conduct" cases, one may then ask another question: Are there any patterns to be found in this activity, any types of cases where the lawyers are particularly likely to make special efforts? It may be remembered that one such uniformity in conduct cases had to do with the type of violation suspected: Offenses that attorneys found personally objectionable moved them to special efforts. The analogous consideration in mergers is size. Just as there are some mergers that are prima facie "too small" for the lawyers to investigate, so too are there mergers among companies so large that their acquisitions are automatically investigated and seriously challenged no matter how innocent they seem on their face.

The exact effect of the lawyers' animus against bigness is hard to measure. The division is by no means engaged in a single-minded attack on the nation's largest firms. In part this dispersion of energies can be explained by the nature of the information the division receives and by the staff's desire to bring the cases it *can* bring: Most of the time, the complaint or notice at hand does not concern Exxon, IBM, or AT&T. But it is true that when a case involving a very large firm comes to the division's attention, the lawyers' suspicion will spur them to shape principles that will reach these cases.

So what is "big"? There is no single standard the lawyers say they apply. Other things being equal, an acquisition by a firm with fifty million dollars in annual sales and a clear 50 percent of its market will be of more interest as a potential case than an acquisition by a seventy-five-million-dollar firm with a 10 percent market share. To be sure, a lawyer may take special interest in a merger for reasons other than size or market share alone. But in the above examples of "new" arguments, the lawyer was dealing either with a local market monopolized by one firm or with a company in the Fortune 500.

The lawyers' evaluations of the importance of absolute size vary. But the following statement by one lawyer is a fair summary of prevailing staff attitudes:

Usually, we look at market concentration more than at absolute size. For instance, in the _____ merger I was telling you about, [Firm A] was the number-two firm in a market where the top two firms had 85 percent. And [Firm B] was third in the market. But I would say we *are* more concerned about larger firms. For instance in banking, we won't look at acquisitions under ten million dollars, though we'll lower it some if the market is very small and localized. But with smaller firms, you always have to pay attention to the size of the market. Not with the bigger companies so much. For instance, you take the conglomerates. Absolute size is why we've been so innovative there. . . . If I had to name an absolute level where I'm *really* going to go all out to get them, I'd say that the Fortune 500 is the trigger.

Thus when dealing with an acquisition by a relatively small firm, the lawyers profess themselves more willing to accept concentration levels, market definitions, and the possible range of anticompetitive effects as given. A large firm will encourage them to find new definitions of concentration levels and markets and new varieties of anticompetitive effects.

But the impact of the lawyers' views on bigness or other such factors is limited by the ad hoc nature of their inventions. In the absence of a particular case, they seem not to spend time thinking about where the law should be going or where the economy needs more competition. There are exceptions; a few lawyers in the division do think along these lines. One of them defined his list of future antitrust targets in this way: " . . . lawyers' fee-fixing, the NAB code—there are thousands of these things. Some are legitimate—but for instance, what about the TV advertising boycotts on contraceptives and hard liquor? And the rule that they can't disparage each other's products?" And not just individuals but some special sections of the division—the patents unit, for instance—have a comparably clear notion of how they would change antitrust law in their areas.

But a more typical lawyer, when asked for his own antitrust agenda, sighed and said, "You just don't have time to sit around and think about busting up GM." The lawyers extend their reach by meeting the particular cases before them and the problems these entail. The staff attorney who thought to extend the Sherman Act in his particular industry, when asked whether he worried about the legal confusion that might result, seemed unconcerned. "Lawyers take their cases as given," he said, "and try to broaden their reach, without worrying whether the trend is 'neat.'"

So far the lawyers' decision rules have been described as follows: Most of their work is cut-and-dried, specified by current antitrust law. When they receive information about a clearly prohibited situation, they invariably recommend prosecution. More often, because the conduct involved does not violate the law or because they cannot prove a violation in court, they recommend against prosecution. They encounter two major kinds of ambiguity: tenuous evidence and tenuous theory. (Even where they admit ambiguities, though, they usually recommend prosecution.) One response they make to ambiguity is to invent new ways of gathering evidence and new theories under which conduct may be deemed anticompetitive. They make special efforts of this type when they are dealing with a suspected violation that seems especially predatory, when a market is very concentrated, or when a firm is very large. But these predilections do not have as much influence as they might because the lawyers approach cases ad hoc, not in light of definite larger notions of the proper direction of antitrust law and enforcement.

In other words the lawyers follow the maxim "When in doubt, prosecute." Yet this is still an incomplete description of what they do. Of the cases investigated "seriously," prosecution is recommended in fewer than half; most of the rejections occur because the case cannot possibly be won. But not all cases are so unambiguous, and not all the ambiguous cases are met by a new invention and a positive recommendation. Perhaps the most interesting decisions the lawyers make occur when they decide not to prosecute even though relief is possible and the case might be won.

The Decision Not to Prosecute

It must be emphasized how few these situations are. Most of time, the lawyers are of the opinion that cases that can be won will have good effects. A typical attitude was expressed by the lawyer who wanted the division to prosecute the television industry for its boycott of liquor advertisements. When asked about possible undesirable effects of such prosecution, the lawyer answered, "Things

like that—and unemployment, and pollution—aren't my problem
. . . . Antitrust has enough to do. . . . And besides, a commissar is
never as successful at any of these things as a free market." Several
lawyers said they would rather have an attorney general who
turned down an occasional case for purely partisan political reasons than one who systematically balanced proposed antitrust
prosecutions against competing economic or social goals.

But self-censorship does sometimes occur, though never without soul-searching by the investigating lawyer and debate within
the staff. One set of reasons the lawyers give for such self-censorship may be classified under the heading of "bad economic
effects." One lawyer told how he had recommended not to prosecute a certain merger even though the case was winnable and, as
he said, "the acquiring firm was one of America's largest manufacturing firms." His reason was that the merger was actually procompetitive—that it would turn the acquired firm from an insignificant
competitor in its industry into a potent challenger to the market's
dominant firms. It was not that the lawyer thought that he lacked a
winnable case. It was instead his conviction that winning the case
would have bad effects on competition in the economy.

This type of argument appears most frequently when the lawyers
deal with industries dominated by one or a few very large firms.
One lawyer told why he had recommended against challenging a
merger between the third and fifth largest firms in a market of
which well over two-thirds was held by a single giant. "You have to
give these other guys an opportunity to compete better," he said.
"It's kind of funny to be attacking them when you leave Number
One alone."

Opinions of this type are never unanimous. In every case in
which a lawyer reported that he was against prosecution for such
reasons, another lawyer could be found who had recommended
the opposite—on the grounds, to take the example above, that

there could be two kinds of effects on competition. First, there
could be more competition for Number One. But Number One
has over two-thirds of the market already; what difference does it
make whether Number Two has 5 percent or 10 percent? But second, what's the effect on the _____ remaining . . . companies?
Will it trigger other mergers and make it harder for them to com-

pete? Will it be harder for them to get money? . . . I thought it should be challenged.

But even apart from the existence of debate among colleagues, what is interesting is that lawyers did not speak of turning down cases on economic grounds without misgivings. Arguments from economics were rarely enough to make them feel content with a decision to recommend against prosecution.

If the lawyers occasionally debate general questions of competition and economic health, such debates are infrequent compared to another type of reason they give for not bringing a case: their concern for the well-being of one specific competitor or group of competitors. One lawyer said that he had "turned down" a case involving cooperative advertising of a single product by a group of small independent businessmen, even though it was clear to him that this common advertising also entailed price-fixing. It was a violation, the lawyer thought, but "they just might not survive otherwise." In this case the law seemed to demand prosecution; indeed, economic reasoning might have recommended against allowing these small retailers to survive. But, the attorney said, he had not been thinking systematically of economic effects; he simply did not like to see small firms going out of business "in this age of . . . concentration."

Another lawyer revealed a similarly protective attitude toward small businesses. The case involved a clear discrimination in services to groups of small users of a certain large facility. Some of these small users complained to the division, claiming that they should have the right to buy the services available to larger firms. On purely legal grounds the case seemed clear enough, but, the staff attorney pointed out, the withdrawal of some participants from the special program for small users might lead the company to discontinue the program altogether, and "I wouldn't want to be responsible for raising prices for all the other little guys."

This concern for small business occasionally intrudes even into cases involving criminal violations. One lawyer gave his own favorite candidate for the category of "cases I don't like to bring." The division had ironclad evidence, he said, of a price-fix among small growers of a certain agricultural commodity:

But we decided not to bring it. After all, those guys were only making _____ dollars a year from this thing. . . . It's not just that they're small. It's like the _____ growers in _____—with weather and blights. It's where people are subject to external influences. It's still partly an economic decision, but. . . . For instance, there was a case like this, the _____ fishermen off the _____ Coast. The guy did bring that one, but he had great misgivings.

So one tendency toward leniency appears in cases where prosecution might harm small businessmen, especially small businessmen with certain natural disadvantages, whether or not they "deserve" prosecution or protection in legal or economic terms. But there is one other kind of misgiving that the lawyers often express about "winnable" cases. It occurs when the case involves a product the lawyer thinks is of great social importance. One such case involved a merger that the investigating lawyer thought to be on the whole anticompetitive but that he thought held out the promise of hastening development of a product that would radically reduce one kind of environmental pollution. "When I finally wrote the memo," he remembered his recommendation, "I said that what was most important was that the _____ be developed quickly. If it could be developed under competitive circumstances, so much the better, but the development was paramount." Similarly, another lawyer explained why he was reluctant to bring a case involving a clear tie-in between a piece of machinery and a certain product necessary to its operation. "The problem is its being in the medical field," he said. "The machine is subsidizing the accessory product, and if they were untied, the price of the product would rise, at least in the short run. Those things are expensive enough as it is, and they're so vital. . . . "

As with the case of the giant-dominated industry mentioned above, this lawyer's argument did not go undisputed by his colleagues. Another lawyer who had worked on this same case mentioned it independently when he was making the argument that the division should *not* allow short-run sympathies like this one to deter it from the pursuit of the long-run benefits that would result from maximum competition.

Thus the lawyers give three major types of reasons for hesitating to bring a case they think they can win. The lawyer might be persuaded that prosecution would have anticompetitive effects, might harm a small or struggling businessman, or could prevent or slow the dissemination of an important commodity. The range of these mitigating factors is narrow; they do not often prove decisive to a staff attorney, and when they do, they are sure to elicit opposing opinions from at least some of his colleagues. It is not hard to see why this is so; the staff lawyers are rewarded for exercising their ingenuity to bring new cases, not to stop them.

This chapter has argued that to describe the division staff's operating principles, one must first describe the current state of antitrust case law: Except for a few senior lawyers, the staff spends most of its time on investigations whose results are unambiguous with respect to the law or the evidence needed to prove its violation. Beyond this description, one may say that when a lawyer thinks a practice anticompetitive or "bad" but beyond the reach of the present law, a frequent reaction is to try to extend the law to cover it. Because of the ad hoc nature of these attempts, it is hard to describe exactly when they will occur except to say that they are more likely when lawyers are dealing with very large firms or with what they suspect is conscious predatory intent. Needless to say, decisions not to bring a possibly winnable case are even more idiosyncratic and much less frequent. A businessman being investigated by the division might in theory persuade a staff lawyer not to prosecute for one of the mitigating reasons listed above, but he would be ill-advised to stake too much on the possibility of such persuasion.

The attitudes and models that one observes among division staff attorneys are, then, reflected in the principles by which they decide particular cases: The impulse toward prosecution is strong, while considerations that would mitigate it are rare, idiosyncratic, and rarely undisputed. But even this more detailed description of the staff lawyers' operating principles is only a partial account of the division's final product in this area—its list of cases actually filed. It ignores at least two important phenomena. In the first place, not all cases the staff recommends for prosecution are accepted by the front office. And second, the division does sometimes act not on an exclusively case-by-case basis but in the context of a more systematic campaign against some offense, economic situation, or prevailing interpretation of the law. These phenomena raise two major questions: What criteria does the front office use to make its decisions on these cases? And what are the source and nature of these more systematic efforts at prosecution? The next two chapters will discuss these questions.

Functions of the Executive: Review

The preceding chapters have described the way Antitrust staff lawyers receive their information, choose subjects for investigation, and recommend whether a prosecution be instituted. The lawyers themselves think that they exercise substantial independence in doing these jobs. It is possible, though, that this perception is inaccurate. Higher-level personnel might screen information in ways the staff is not aware of, or staff decisions might be relatively unimportant because they are so often overruled. One can begin to see whether this is the case by looking more directly at the executive levels of the organization—to see how the division hierarchy distributes information to the lawyers, how it supervises the staff during investigations, and how often and why it overrules staff recommendations on whether to prosecute. This chapter will ask these questions of routine decisions within the division; special campaigns against some offense, industry, or interpretation of the law will be discussed later on. The question to be asked of the more routine supervision is "To what extent does the executive change the division's output from what it would be if decisions were made on the basis of the staff lawyers' criteria alone?"

Supervision of the division's staff is carried out at three levels. Most of the staff lawyers themselves are assigned to distinct sections, each of which has responsibility for a number of commodities or functions not always closely related to one another. Each section is supervised first by a section chief and his assistant. The section chiefs, in turn, report to the director of operations, whose office also contains an assistant director and a small staff. The director of operations is responsible in turn to the assistant attorney general, who is assisted by deputies and a personal staff. Also reporting to the AAG, and coequal with the director of operations, is a director of policy planning, who supervises a planning staff, an evaluations section with its own section chief, and various special-purpose sections. The policy planning director may comment on recommendations for prosecution, and his comment carries weight. But unlike the director of operations, he has at most times not routinely commented on every case.

Each of these supervisors has several opportunities to influence the outcome of investigations. The section chief disseminates the initial information to his staff; he can be in constant contact with them during the course of an investigation; and he must add his recommendation to theirs when a matter goes forward to the front office. The director's office, in turn, disseminates information to the section chiefs; it formally supervises the chiefs during investigations; and it adds its own recommendation when a case goes forward to the assistant attorney general's office. The AAG's office takes no routine part in the collection and dissemination of information, but if matters worthy of investigation come to its attention, it can of course send them on to the staff through the director and section chiefs. Furthermore, it can always intervene in an investigation, and the AAG makes the division's final decisions on prosecution.

The Section Chiefs: Information

Of these supervisors, it is the section chiefs who exercise by far the closest watch over the trial attorneys. The chiefs' formal responsibilities are to distribute work among the staff lawyers; to supervise them while they are investigating and trying cases; to approve, amend, or disapprove their briefs and recommendations; to participate in decisions regarding their salaries and promotions; and to mediate between them and the higher echelons.

The section chiefs are usually chosen from among the trial lawyers themselves. A major standard of selection seems to be the same criterion by which staff lawyers judge their colleagues: their reputation and record as able, successful prosecuting attorneys. Almost none of the section chiefs is considered incompetent in this respect; no one without some reputation for professional competence, it is rightly thought, could establish any authority over his subordinates.

But not every good prosecutor can become a section chief; a successful candidate must satisfy further criteria. Some of these are the obvious ones: The candidate must have some presumptive ability to keep administrative records, to organize, to get along with subordinates and superiors. Blatantly abrasive personalities do not become section chiefs, or at the very least are usually passed over for some time before an offer is made to them. Particular section chiefs may be chosen to supply what the front office thinks the division needs at a particular time. For instance, if it is thought that a section needs an infusion of "youth" in its outlook, the next chief might well be relatively young in age and even younger in manner. Or a clique in a particular section might be causing friction; if so, the ability to conciliate or to be firm in the allocation of work might become crucial in the selection of a chief.

But there is a further and especially important similarity among the section chiefs. They express, are seen as holding, and are thought to have held before their promotion a particular care for what lawyers refer to as the "soundness" of the division's "product" and for the details of that product. This is not to say that the section chiefs seem to be chosen for any special theoretical unadventurousness or lack of prosecutorial zeal. But the chiefs, it is thought, must be persons whose instinct is to ensure that the division not pursue other goals at the cost of its reputation for professional skill and meticulousness. The chiefs, in other words, have as part of their job the task of protecting a commitment in the division to legal craftsmanship.

There is some overt competition for the job, but less than one might expect. The relative dearth stems partly from the fact that vacancies are often not announced until a replacement has already been chosen, but there are other reasons as well. The job's advantages are three: the chance to move into the post of director of operations (the highest position that a career lawyer usually attains), higher salary, and, for those with a taste for it, the pleasures of administrative power. But from a trial lawyer's point of view there is also a serious disadvantage to the job of section chief. At least in theory, a section chief must give up his own litigation. In fact, some chiefs refuse to abandon their work as litigators completely, but they do have to cut back significantly. This disadvantage does not prevent people from wanting the job, but it does seem to give pause and thus to lessen the intensity of competition. It has also caused some section chiefs to resign and return to trial work, and it seriously affects the chiefs' behavior while in office.

The section chiefs have their first opportunity to influence the handling of cases when matters are assigned within the division. As was described in the preceding chapter, information comes to the division principally in the forms of complaints from citizens, busi-

nessmen, or government officials; data from business publications; and personal contacts or observations by division lawyers.
In the first two cases, all information goes through the office of the
director of operations and is parceled out to the appropriate section chiefs.

The director's office professes to do almost no preliminary
screening of this information; it merely distributes matters to the
appropriate sections. The man in the director's office who supervises this parceling out explained, "We don't do any of that [dis-
carding information] at this level. . . . I have girls receiving the
mail, clipping the press. . . . We just route it to the section chiefs.
They do the selection."

Usually there is no question about which section chief should
get a piece of information. Each section handles its list of commodities or types of commerce, and a matter concerning one of them
will go to the section that normally handles it. Questions of jurisdiction arise occasionally. A matter might involve two different
commodities in two different sections or, less frequently, an item
may "belong" according to commodity in Section A, but the legal
issue involved may already be under extensive consideration in
Section B. In either of these situations, the matter will be given to
each section chief who might have an interest, so that each chief
can tell the director's office whether he would like his section to
handle it. If only one chief expresses an interest, there is no conflict to be resolved. More rarely—in perhaps six to a dozen matters
a year, it was reported—two or more chiefs do want the item.

The director's office seems to settle disputes on the basis of two
principles. One is availability of staff time. If a matter looks as
though it might be important, it is crucial that a section have
enough manpower free in the immediate future—including an
able senior lawyer—to handle it. Beyond this logistical standard,
disputed cases are allocated by logrolling. A section chief who lost
possession of the last case will have a special claim on the director
in the next one.

These relatively rare frontal disputes by no means constitute a
continuing major conflict within the organization. But there is
some competition among the section chiefs for the "good" cases,
especially mergers and price-fixings involving large companies. If a

section chief can manage to find out about such matters before the director's office informs all the chiefs officially, he can get his claim in first and thus, he thinks, have an impact on the disposition of the desired cases. Therefore, one section chief explained,

> . . . the significant stuff, we *know* about. I read the *Wall Street Journal* every morning. . . . They do clip it for us in the director's office, but *that* doesn't come until the afternoon. And meanwhile the FTC [Federal Trade Commission] might get clearance for it, or some other section chief might get it. I *fight* to get those good cases for my section.

The section chiefs also take pride, just as the staff lawyers do, in the matters they can generate for their sections through their own contacts, past experience, and contextual knowledge of their sections' industries. One section chief was defending the proposition that the division's general organization by commodities was superior to the alternative plan of organizing it according to "functions," such as categories of offense. Functional organization "isn't effective," he said:

> For instance, we have _____ and _____ equipment in this section. We got a routine letter from a U.S. attorney for an [association] in one town, asking whether a group of them could buy a building and rent space in it to a _____ laboratory. Sounded innocent. But I remembered that we had had a case ten years ago where we got a judgment against a bunch of [them] for monopolizing _____ laboratories. It didn't take me long to find out that this guy had been one of the defendants. . . .

Thus while the section chiefs do not often fight over cases in the director's office, they have other ways of expressing their enthusiasm for getting more and better cases. They, like the trial lawyers, see the availability of enforcement opportunities as a situation of scarcity.

Once they have received information, the section chiefs decide whether an item merits consideration. Two sorts of items do not get passed along to a trial lawyer. First there are a few matters that the section chiefs and their assistants keep for themselves, usually cases in their own particular specialities. "I still do some of my own litigation now," one of them put it. "I don't think the front office likes it—but it's something I don't want to give up. Certainly I *hope* they don't consider me an administrator."

More common are items that are literally thrown into the waste-basket. The section chief initials office records to show that he has read an item, then throws it away. Or, in the case of a complaint, he has the letter answered by his own office without sending it to a staff lawyer for investigation.

When one asks the section chiefs what gets thrown away and why, one finds that the criteria are the same in form as, but even more lenient than, the staff lawyers': Anything that could possibly result in a case is kept. The section chiefs do not think of them-selves as exercising discretion at this stage, and they throw things out for the same reasons the lawyers do: The offense complained of is not an offense, or the company is too small, or it has no market power and little chance of achieving any. Otherwise, the matter is handed on.

The section chiefs explain why they do not exercise more judg-ment over what gets handed out for investigation. One reason is that they are unwilling to give up the chance of finding a case when cases are not easy to find. Another reason is that investigating even "doubtful" pieces of information helps to train young lawyers. And there is yet a third reason for their not wanting to be, as one of them described it, "too conservative." They want the division not only to be zealous and diligent in enforcement but also to seem to be zealous and diligent. One section chief explained:

. . . many times I have to make a decision to investigate because the chances are that it's not a case, but we would have to avoid complaints because it *looks* like an obvious case. We get lots of these in the merger field. Many times, we investigate thoroughly, and it's a close one; and the decision is made not to sue. When I see another merger in the same field that's even smaller, then a fortiori it's not going to be a case. But I know I can't justify my decision on this alone. . . . I know there'll be mail. So I do look at it—but I use young lawyers.

Similarly, the section chiefs exercise only limited discretion when they decide how to allocate items among the staff lawyers. Their criteria for answering the question of who gets what seem fairly simple. The first is the perceived experience and competence of individual lawyers: A piece of information that looks "good" —in terms of both the likelihood of gathering the appropriate evi-dence and the amount of commerce involved—will go to a senior lawyer who is well thought of (and the section chiefs tend to think well of roughly the same people that the staff lawyers do). Another criterion is available time, and the third is the lawyers' own preferences and fields of expertise. Some lawyers prefer work in certain industries, others like particular kinds of offenses (for example, criminal rather than civil). As far as one can tell, there is no conscious effort to use this allocation process to "favor" any particular offense, industry, or theory.

When a lawyer who looks at this information tells his section chief that he would like to launch an investigation, he is almost always given permission to do so. The division does not keep statistics on this point, but trial lawyers and section chiefs say that 90 to 95 percent of requests for investigations are authorized. "Investigations?" one section chief asked rhetorically. "I guess I'm too liberal about authorizing them. I guess I should be more hard-nosed, but I figure if a guy wants to do something, I should let him do it." The overriding considerations in allowing investigations to go forward are, first, that the staff's professional judgments must be presumed trustworthy, and, second, that so much information is useless for purposes of prosecution that one cannot afford to overlook possible opportunities. Again, the assumption is that in an environment of scarcity, case possibilities should not be neglected.

In sum, the staff lawyers are essentially correct in believing that no one in the division makes very deliberate decisions about incoming information before they themselves do. The director's office views itself as an information collector and disseminator, not as a screen. The section chiefs, far from rejecting information from the director's office, compete to maximize information and supplement the officially provided information with their own. Moreover, the section chiefs say that they deliberately err on the side of liberality in handing information on to their staffs and authorizing investigations. They use a quick version of the same criteria the staff uses when deciding the probable worth of an item. Because they genuinely want to find cases, because they want to give the impression of diligence, and because they want to train young lawyers, their rule seems to be, "When in doubt, investigate." There have been times in recent years when the prosecutorial business at hand has more than fully occupied the staff. But the result has been delay and backlog, not any permanent change in decision criteria and procedures.

It could be argued that the section chiefs' screening procedures do in fact influence the outcome of investigations by giving the most problematic cases to the least experienced lawyers. A more experienced lawyer, after all, should be better able to find the case in whatever comes his way. But in fact, precisely because the younger lawyers are unlikely to be put in charge of a matter that looks obviously important, these younger lawyers are especially eager for cases of their own. Therefore when a section chief hands a doubtful matter to a younger lawyer, he is giving it to the individual who has the most powerful incentive to carry out an energetic investigation. The section chief may strongly suspect what the outcome of a matter will be, but his decisions between older and younger lawyers do not ensure that outcome.

The Section Chiefs: Investigations

Distributing information is not the only or even the major chance that the section chiefs have to determine the ultimate outcome of investigations. They can also exercise direction and control by their demands and suggestions during the course of the investigations themselves. And in fact the chiefs do exercise this kind of influence. Each of the section chiefs interviewed pointed out that because all correspondence to and from the staff lawyers during an investigation passes through a section chief's office, he knows in some detail how each investigation is progressing. In addition, the chiefs are responsible to the front office for a formal monthly report on each pending investigation.

But it is more than the necessity for monthly reports that stirs the supervisory interest of the section chiefs, and more than the lawyers' correspondence that supplies them with information. There is little doubt that the section chiefs feel personally responsible for their sections' progress and products, and there is equally little doubt that the chiefs encourage the greatest possible contact with their staffs. Each section chief or assistant section chief interviewed said, in almost identical words, "People don't have to make an appointment to see me. I have an 'open door' policy."

This policy seems to be successful; communication with the staff lawyers is frequent. Some of the lawyers, it is true, claim not to see their section chiefs even once in several weeks, but these are usually young lawyers working under senior lawyers on major cases, cases about which the senior lawyer does the major part of the talking to the section chief and front office. More lawyers say—and say truthfully, to judge from the traffic in and out of the section chiefs' offices—that they see their section chiefs "all the time." Sometimes they are called in to discuss the progress of an investigation or a piece of writing that they have produced, but they also go on their own initiative. And they claim to take this initiative not mainly because they think the section chiefs would somehow be offended or exercise sanctions if not approached with new information and requests for advice (though this consideration may not be entirely absent from their minds) but because they think the section chiefs can be useful to them in their work.

The section chiefs, in other words, wield an authority of expertise rather than only the authority of office. They are looked upon as experienced craftsmen. The section chiefs vary in their reputations, but with the exception of one chief, the lawyers spoke of their section chiefs' legal abilities with admiration or at least approval. The only systematically adverse comments come from the young lawyers in some sections who feel that their section chiefs are too conservative in their attitude toward extending the law to cover relatively new or doubtful cases, too quick to see distinctions that refute the analogies the young lawyers present to them. But even those who complain in this way almost invariably add as a coda (and add more than formulaically, it would seem, since they do not seem systematically reticent about expressing their likes and dislikes) that the section chief is "really solid" or "really knows his stuff." So the question to be considered is not whether the division is run laissez-faire style by the section chiefs; it is not. The question is rather that of the uses to which all this communication and authority are put.

The first point to be made is that each section contains a number of senior lawyers who talk to the section chiefs often, as friends and valued colleagues, but whose judgments are seldom questioned by the chief. Some of this confidence displayed by the chiefs is the result of simple deference. But by far the more important reason—and the reason why these senior lawyers are important to the division in the first place—is that in the section chiefs' eyes these lawyers are simply very able. The chiefs think that the decisions these lawyers make are the same ones a section chief himself would make if he were as well acquainted with the case in question. One section chief was explaining the kinds of changes he usually made in his lawyers' work; then he added, naming two of the senior lawyers, "Of course there are exceptions, _____ and _____, I hardly have to touch their stuff." These lawyers, to a large extent, run their own investigations.

Most lawyers get more advice than this, more requests for information during investigations, and more challenges to and editing of their work. By the accounts of both section chiefs and staff lawyers, the great majority of this advice is what an outsider would call technical—not unimportant, certainly, since cases turn on such things, but in areas whose very discussion assumes an agreement not only about general purposes but also about fairly specific goals and means. When one asks the lawyers themselves what kinds of advice or questions they usually get from their section chiefs, the first specific example they give almost invariably concerns some legal or administrative procedure. For instance:

It's _____'s policy to ask you what you've been doing if you haven't turned up anything in four months. . . . What he does do is make you do the chores that aren't so interesting. Right now I have a memo I'm supposed to write that'll take about one day, on an investigation that didn't pan out. Of course I'd rather work on something good than spend the day on something that I'm recommending I never see again.

Or, on a level slightly more elevated than that of keeping the paper moving:

_____ said I shouldn't just send them a request for information; I should ask for a grand jury instead, because these guys *did* know what they were doing. Reciprocity is *known* to be an offense by now. And a request for information will just make them say they'll stop doing whatever they've been doing.

Besides such matters of administration and tactics, those lawyers who receive advice from their section chiefs report that the major category of instruction consists of hints on how to investigate, how and where to find information and offenses in ways and places the attorney may not have considered. One lawyer described such advice by saying, "You try things out on your section chief. Often he'll come up with suggestions for further investigation." Another lawyer observed, "The section chiefs are good. They give good hints. . . . You can be talking to _____ and he'll introduce something you haven't even *thought* of."

The section chiefs themselves agree with this notion of what their major job is during investigations: to prod the less experienced, zealous, or inventive lawyers into rooting out all the possible evidence of violations in a given matter and to ensure that they make the best possible use of the legal tools at their disposal. "I call someone in," one of them described his work, "and say, 'What's the matter? Don't you know a tie-in when you see one?'" And another explained, "At each stage of the game they give me memos, and I ask for more information—so eventually they get a case. . . . Something generally *is* there if something has gone on for very long."

During investigation, the section chiefs refrain from making final judgments on the worth of a possible case, especially negative ones. Instead, they perform three other functions. First, they make sure that the lawyers do their work "right"—in the sense of performing purely bureaucratic chores and in the sense of conforming to certain technical requirements of legal craftsmanship. Second, they discuss questions of tactics—not mainly of whether a case should be prosecuted in some form but what form, civil or criminal, with what defendants, according to which particular theory, might be most successful. As will be discussed later, still more of this type of discussion goes on as the investigation nears the stage of final recommendation. Finally, the section chiefs try to help each investigation reach a positive conclusion by giving practical advice on investigative technique and asking questions about overlooked ways in which a prospective defendant might be in violation of the law. In short, during investigations the section chiefs overwhelmingly use their expertise and authority to promote cases, not to discourage them. This is not to say that the chiefs are never discouraging; but, in general, the division adage that "It's ten times easier to open an investigation around here than it is to close one" reflects not only the chiefs' leniency about opening investigations but their behavior during the course of investigations as well. The section chiefs have considerable influence over the staff, but during investigations they do not use this influence in behalf of goals sharply different from those shared by the trial lawyers themselves.

The Section Chiefs: The Decision to Prosecute

The last stage at which the section chiefs have an opportunity to influence both the decision to prosecute and the type and manner of prosecution is the preparation of the final memorandum to the front office. In this memo, the investigating lawyers recommend a case or not; if they recommend one, they will ask for a grand jury or attach a copy of a proposed complaint. This final memo must go through the section chief's office and receive his recommendation as well.

The first point to be made about these recommendations by the section chiefs is that most decisions on whether to prosecute are consensual. In a large majority of cases, the existence of a violation and the proper course of action were never in question at all, or they were decided long before a recommendation was made. There are the lawyers whose word a section chief will simply accept in these matters; there are those he has prodded until their results satisfy him; and there is the preexisting consensus among division members that some things clearly constitute a case and some things do not. These agreed-upon cases are recommended or, more often, closed out with no disagreement and little discussion.

Even in cases where a recommendation to prosecute and the major strategy to be used are agreed upon by all parties, the section chief will usually amend the written product involved. Indeed, it is the amendment process, rather than passing a yes-or-no judgment on staff recommendations, that the section chiefs consider their major function at this advanced stage. Both staff lawyers and section chiefs agree that with the exception of work by the few "autonomous" lawyers, almost nothing leaves the chiefs' offices unchanged—in the form of the complaint, or the defendants named, or the relief sought. As one chief explained his job,

Reviewing things is my biggest administrative job. I have to make sure the theory is okay, and the facts, and the recommendation. Here's a proposed complaint. I *never* send that up unchanged. For instance, I might call someone in and ask, "What do you mean to accomplish by this paragraph?" . . . my job is to see that things leave here in the best possible shape. Like this stuff—I'll spend half a day rewriting it. Sometimes it's more editing than criticism.

Another man summarized what goes on in these rewritings: "Lots of this is professional pride. When I came here, the Antitrust Division was the *cream*. And we try to keep it that way, even to the commas. . . . We have to have a reputation for being solid." The point here is not that such changes are "unimportant"; it is rather that they rarely have to do with the decision on whether or not to bring a case in the first place.

Thus in the majority of cases, the question of the section chief's ability to reverse the staff does not arise because there is no disagreement on the major issue of whether to prosecute. The chief conceives of his major job as the critical and editorial task of ensuring that the written product is as rigorous as he can make it in argument and detail.

But such unanimity is not always the case. There are several kinds of recurring disagreements between section chiefs and staff. Rarest is the situation in which the lawyers on an investigation finally recommend closing it without a prosecution, but the chief thinks a case does exist in the data and resists closing it. One section chief tried to think of examples in this category and then simply concluded, "It's hard to recall a case like this." The lawyers want to bring cases; it is unlikely that at least one staff lawyer will not have as aggressive a view as the section chief's. And the section chief has already had many opportunities to probe for the additional information that might support a positive feeling on his part.

But the situation does occur occasionally, and, when it does, the section chief will almost invariably acquiesce in the staff decision, even if he has his doubts. In the first place, he knows that the lawyers are usually eager to prosecute; he may suspect that in the matter at hand they were not clever enough to find the way to do so, but at least he knows that he is not dealing with any systematic leniency on their part. Moreover, each investigation is built on many documents and interviews. Only those who have actually read the documents, the section chiefs think, can have a comprehensive and detailed knowledge about the facts. If such persons say there is no evidence of a violation, it might take a complete rereading to prove the opposite. One section chief mentioned a long investigation in his section that had been closed in this way and said, "I wasn't satisfied. But you can't second-guess; you have to accept the lawyer's evaluation of what the *facts* are."

Much more frequent are the cases where the staff recommends positively or is split but the section chief for some reason disapproves the case. The chiefs' reports of what proportion of the staff recommendations fall into this category ranged from a low of 20 percent to a high of 40 percent. The low "reject" estimates came from the chiefs who displayed a more generally aggressive prosecutorial attitude and who specially emphasized their close and continuous contacts with the staff in the stages of investigation prior to the final staff recommendation.

It is hard to see, from examples that the lawyers or the section chiefs give, much in the way of patterns in the kinds of cases the chiefs are most likely to disapprove—by size, or industry, or type of offense. But there are two exceptions to this seeming randomness. First, the lawyers reported that the most frequent reason for disapproval was the quality of the evidence; a section chief simply did not think that a court would believe the division's case. And second, lawyers reported that recommendations were turned down when they had tried to extend a previous court decision to cover a new instance of similar but not identical behavior; a section chief would argue that the distinction was important enough to cause the division to lose in court.

Thus if there is a consideration the section chiefs defend with more vigor than the trial lawyers, it is the desire to maintain the division's reputation as an organization that does not bring cases lightly, or badly prepared, or unsuccessfully. The same "professional pride" that makes the section chiefs edit the lawyers' work until they think it "solid," "even to the commas," makes them more reluctant than the staff to take a chance on a doubtful case.

But one should not exaggerate the extent of this difference between the section chiefs and the staff. By far the majority of the criteria the chiefs profess to use in their decisions are the lawyers' own. Moreover, the chiefs, too, are eager to find cases, authorize investigations, and ensure that these investigations bear prosecutorial fruit. As one lawyer put it, "It's not the section chiefs who give you the trouble. After all, they're 'in on it' to some extent." Finally, even when a section chief does have some doubts about a case, he will often respond in a way that shows considerable deference to the staff lawyers' professional judgment, independence, and desire to prosecute.

For one thing, when there is a disagreement among the staff or between section chief and staff, the chief frequently tries to forge a compromise that will command unanimous support and allow prosecution to go forward in some form. If a case is recommended as a criminal prosecution and the chief thinks the evidence is not strong enough, he may secure the staff's agreement to a civil case. Or, as one of them explained, "Sometimes we'll drop a defendant, sometimes we'll drop a count." Finding an agreed-upon formula was important, he went on: "We *do* come to a consensus; you *need* it to get through the front office."

The reason this section chief gave for the need to come to consensus—to get a case approved by the higher echelons—is evidence that the section chiefs feel at least as much loyalty toward their prosecuting attorneys as they do toward the front office. The positive recommendations from the staff end up being few enough —"About 5 percent of the things I send out finally come back with a positive recommendation," one chief estimated—and the chiefs' sense of obligation toward their lawyers strong enough so that section chiefs do not reverse staff recommendations lightly. There will invariably be extended discussions between the chief and the staff, and according to all reports, these are discussions in which not only staff but section chiefs as well feel constrained to defend their positions.

It is true that all opinions in these discussions are not quite equal; the section chief's opinion carries more weight with the front office. But this weight is not so great as to give any chief an absolute veto. No section chief ever closes a case wholly on his own authority—that is, without sending all conflicting opinions to the front office for adjudication—unless the staff lawyers consent. Where there is a difference of opinion, the chief gives the opposing memoranda to the director of operations. And if a staff lawyer feels strongly enough about a case, he knows he has the opportunity to try to persuade the director of operations to overrule the chief's recommendation.

This is not to say that the opportunity for appeal is used every time a disagreement occurs or even that it is used very often. But it is used frequently enough so that the lawyers mention it as a real recourse. Some lawyers, it is true, claim that a law of anticipated reactions operates in the division: One stops recommending cases that one knows will not be approved by one's section chief. But this opinion is a minority one. Certainly there is no evidence that section chiefs themselves actively discourage the lawyers from using their opportunity to appeal decisions. In fact the chiefs are fond of emphasizing how "fluid" their "lines of communication" are. They seem quite content to rely on their reputations and persuasion rather than on direct veto power to make their views prevail. As one chief put it, "No one ever achieves a position of power around here where his opinion is unassailable, except of course the assistant attorney general. And that includes me. If one of my staff wants a shot at the director of operations, he gets it." This statement may exaggerate the extent to which staff lawyers feel fully free to make use of their opportunity, but the lawyers by and large agree that section chiefs do not "veto" cases.

So the section chiefs exert a considerable influence over the staff, but they exert it mainly in behalf of principles the staff lawyers themselves share. The chiefs are zealous in finding information of certain kinds, liberal in distributing it, and permissive in authorizing investigations. During the course of these investigations, they act to increase the likelihood that a case will result. When they judge the results of these investigations, they are, not surprisingly, somewhat more skeptical, because somewhat more disinterested, than the staff lawyers are; they also show special concern that the division not bring the cases it is likely to lose. But they often resolve their doubts by finding some consensual formula under which

prosecution can take place, and, when they do reverse their lawyers, they take no steps to close off avenues of appeal.

The Director of Operations

Staff lawyers and section chiefs are alike in viewing the office of the
director as the first locus of genuinely hierarchical authority in the
division. The office of the director has, in theory, authority over all
functions performed by the section chiefs—including the original
parceling out of incoming information and the supervision of investigations. But, as we have seen, the office chooses to exercise
almost no discretion in the former area, except to settle jurisdictional questions with the Federal Trade Commission and to
mediate the occasional dispute about which section gets what investigation. As for the latter area—the investigations themselves
—the office seems to be well enough informed about the progress
of major investigations but does not often feel the need to intervene directly in their course. The assistant director in charge of
these investigations stated, ''We mainly trust the judgment of the
section chiefs about these things.'' So the office's chief influence
on the division's final product lies in its power to decide, after investigations are more or less done, what will get filed and what will
not.

Every case that is recommended for prosecution and every recommendation to close an investigation without prosecuting pass
through the director's office. Within the office, a case is first seen
by the director's staff, which makes its own recommendations on
the matter; it then goes to the director or sometimes the assistant
director for the office's final opinion. The director tends to be a
''career man,'' with experience as staff attorney and section chief
in the division. Formally, he does not make the division's final decision on prosecution; that decision lies with the assistant attorney
general, and in theory—as well as occasionally in practice—a lawyer or section chief can appeal the director's decision to the AAG.
But the clear consensus in the division is that the director's opinion
is more equal than that of anyone but the AAG himself; his decisions carry a great deal of weight. What is in question is not the fact
of his influence but, once again, the uses to which it is put.

As with the section chiefs, the usual situation when a case is recommended for prosecution or closing is agreement among all parties—staff, section chief, and operations office. And the office's rate of agreement with the section chiefs alone (whether or not the chiefs agree with their staffs) seems even higher. "We approve well over 50 percent of the recommendations for complaints," one of the director's assistants said. "I wouldn't say it's nine out of ten —but the chiefs aren't in the habit of making frivolous recommendations." The director himself estimated an even higher rate of approval: "I'd say that in only two cases out of twenty is there a question of whether to bring it—mostly where I say there's no case." So the usual situation is agreement, and, where there is a dispute, it is usually between a section chief who wants to prosecute and the director who does not. As the director put it, "It's *rare* for it to be the other way around, because most people around here want to enforce the law."

What are the reasons for disagreement? The director's assistant summarized, "It could be evidentiary, or because it's too small, or the theory is not clear. But if it gets to the recommendation stage, it's rarely a question of something simply not being a violation of the law." The director himself summarized the categories of disagreement in almost the same words. First of all, he said, "I like to file every case I can. . . . I'm from the old school." But where he does say "no,"

. . . it would probably be because the interstate commerce allegation is thin, or the thing only involves a hundred thousand dollars' worth of commerce, or it's a problem of evidence. It's rare for me to turn something down for policy reasons; these decisions are for the AAG to make—though I would add my own input, a note saying, "I would caution you. . . . "

The assistant director said, "I have no investment in these investigations. . . . All we have to say is, 'Do we have a case? Will we lose the AAG's confidence and destroy our coherence as a legal organization?'"

Thus in virtually all these disputed cases, the director's office claims to turn down the matter for what an outsider would again call technical rather than policy reasons. The reasons do not deal independently with broad economic or social questions; neither do they consciously seek to determine the general direction of antitrust law or policy. These decisions may have the effect, certainly, of determining some general antitrust direction, but such is not usually their purpose. Instead, the director's arguments simply couch themselves in terms of doubt that the case at hand can be won. Even more than the section chiefs, the director's office concerns itself with the division's "coherence as a legal organization," with seeing to it that the division does not lose the cases it brings.

When the staff lawyers describe their conversations with various members of the director's office—on those occasions when bringing a case is seriously in doubt—their accounts of the conversations confirm these impressions. One lawyer, describing his troubles in pushing a case through the front office, recalled: "All _____ kept saying was, 'Show me a case that's ever been brought on this principle.'" And another of these disputes with the front office turned on the following question: "We kept trying to explain to _____ what the case was all about, and all he kept saying was, 'The Federal Power Commission has primary jurisdiction, the FPC has primary jurisdiction.' I finally screamed so hard at him that he left the room." Another young lawyer explained, "If you want, the section chief will send your memo up with a negative recommendation. But this usually won't go beyond the director of operations. He's the key man in this, and he's a career man. . . . So he's tried a lot of cases. And when you want to bring a price-fixing case, he can show you where your evidence won't hold up." In short, the lawyers' stories, both critical and admiring, confirm that the director's office most often makes its decisions according to considerations of procedure, evidence, and, in general, whether a case can be won.

But if the considerations to which the operations office gives conscious attention are mainly of this "nonpolicy" type, it is difficult to describe them in much more systematic detail than that. Certainly the staff lawyers themselves are unable to point to any clear pattern, to any level of size or jurisdictional argument or evidentiary lapse that will almost certainly evoke a "no" from the director's office. By and large, the lawyers profess not to know in advance what combination of factors will tip the balance in a particular case. And to some of them, this is a major source of irritation. One young lawyer expressed his discontent: "Even if a case is disapproved on a higher level, they don't give you any constructive criticism. I asked for an indictment once, and the answer was, 'We can't prove that beyond a reasonable doubt.' What does *that* mean? I've never known what that meant. We should move on probable cause—we're *prosecutors*." All the men interviewed in the director's office agreed that they used very little in the way of precise rules. For instance, one assistant pointed out, "Size is an elusive thing. How 'big' is a million dollars? But maybe it's not just the dollar amount. . . . We have . . . gone on a small amount because of the principle involved, and then there are the price-fixing cases. . . . So many things tip the balance. . . . "

In sum, the director's office, to judge by reports from its members and from the lawyers subject to it, makes its decisions according to what it considers the requirements of legal craft. Indeed, much of its work consists not of making "yes or no" decisions on cases but in making the same kinds of deletions, additions, and corrections the section chiefs make, in another effort to ensure that the case leaves the office in "the best possible shape." "They might be recommending a case," one man in the office said, "and forget to allege interstate commerce. Or I might know of some more decisions that would affect their theories. . . . The 'bad' cases are fixed or weeded out here. Beyond this office, the decisions are made for policy reasons."

Even when these considerations result not merely in reworking a case but in killing it completely, they are considerations of craft rather than of deliberate policy preference. Because they are considerations that derive mainly from accumulated practical experience, it is not surprising that those who use them should be unable to articulate them systematically. And because these considerations are not given any such articulation, it is not surprising that the staff lawyers attached to their particular cases should feel justified in accusing the director's office of being "arbitrary."

But this absence of general rules, and the commitment to treating each case as a unique combination of legal problems, have another effect on the staff, though one it is not so quick to recognize. They reduce to a minimum the extent to which the lawyers can censor themselves in anticipation of the director's reaction.

One simply cannot tell with any great certainty what is sure to be approved or disapproved there. And as long as the possiblity of such self-censorship is small, the lawyers retain their ability to form independently the population of cases from which the director must choose.

The Assistant Attorney General: Final Decisions

"Beyond this office," the director of operations said, "the decisions are made for policy reasons." "Beyond this office" means in the office of the assistant attorney general. It may include a stop at the policy planning section, where, as will be discussed in the next chapter, the criteria for decision have at times been somewhat different from those used by the "operations side." But for most cases, the next people to work on the relevant documents are the assistant attorney general and his staff.

One might expect that decisions here would be made for very different reasons from the reasons at lower levels. Presumably the cases reaching the AAG are all "good" cases—cases involving an appropriately large amount of commerce, "winnable" cases, and cases whose good construction, in terms of both theory and evidence, has been validated by at least six or seven professionals. The AAG's office, therefore, might select among them for their relative importance in light of particular antitrust policy goals.

Selection of this sort does occur. The number of division cases in areas such as mergers has varied under different AAGs. Certain AAGs have explicitly stated that they considered antimonopoly cases too costly to bring in terms of division resources. Certain legal theories and arguments have been rejected by one AAG and accepted by another. Moreover, it will be pointed out in the next chapter that AAGs can have considerable influence in stimulating the staff to bring new types of antitrust cases.

But the effect of final review decisions on the great bulk of antitrust enforcement should not be exaggerated. It is of course possible for an AAG and his staff to decide anew each case that comes before him; some AAGs are reported to have tried to do so. But by far the majority have not. As one director of operations described it, "Your track record, of course, depends on your relationship with the AAG, and how he likes to operate. _____ felt more secure when he made all the decisions. But most of them trust you more; they say, 'He's been around for twenty years.' At *least* 60 percent of these cases, the AAG never even *touches*.''

In other words, the great majority of the cases the division files —or decides not to file—are filed, in effect, on the director's recommendation and in the form in which he approves them. And this 60 or more percent, it is important to note, includes many of the cases that are often cited by outsiders as evidence of a particular, conscious enforcement policy by a particular assistant attorney general.

Even of the 40 percent or less that the AAG's office does "touch," both his office and the director's office agree that perhaps three-quarters are questioned not for their recommendation on whether or not to prosecute but for subsidiary details. When one asks lawyers who have discussed cases with the AAG and his staff what kinds of questions the top office poses to them, the most frequently mentioned are, "Why are you naming this defendant?" and "Should we allege [this] too?"

A member of the AAG's staff remarked of his role in the review process,

This is one of the good things about the division; maybe there are disputes over facts and novel theories, but there are no big policy disputes. Things usually don't come to us as big policy questions.
    I make changes in briefs on an ad hoc basis. Sometimes I see a new argument. This is a large part of the review. . . . Lots of times we're concerned with the pleading, whether the issue is stated well. . . .
    Things come to me where there's a disagreement. . . . I haven't seen any patterns in the disagreements because I haven't had to review that many cases. My view may be asked on a primary jurisdiction question, or a novel Section 2 theory, but I haven't seen enough identical cases to be able to judge. . . .
    I wouldn't say there have been any basic changes in the way I look at these cases from the time I was a staff lawyer; it's just that I don't have lots of investment in the cases any more.

These opinions are interesting in part because they confirm the impression that few of the cases that reach the AAG's office are subjects of major dispute and that a large part of the review that does take place deals with subsidiary questions. But there is a further point to be made about this statement. It suggests that cases an outsider might see as having significant implications for the general direction of antitrust enforcement may in fact be decided in the AAG's office on grounds that are considerably narrower, more technical, and less controversial than one might assume. And there is further, though fragmentary, evidence that such is the case. There is considerable divergence between the significance that press and attentive publics attribute to some well-publicized antitrust cases and the reasons that the decision makers themselves cite as having influenced them in their deliberations. A typical example occurred in a well-publicized conspiracy case against a group of very large manufacturers. The case as finally brought was civil rather than criminal; the division was widely criticized for laxity in enforcement, and it was rumored that the decision was influenced by partisan politics. But one man who had been in the AAG's office at the time remarked of it, "*I* was the one who made the recommendation not to bring a criminal case—not any higher-ups. And I would have liked to bring a criminal case too. But the evidence just wasn't there."

Two categories of cases, then—those not touched at all and those only "tinkered with," as the lawyers put it—seem to comprise the great majority of the AAG's dealings with his subordinates' recommendations. And even of those in which changes are made, such changes are often made on relatively narrow grounds. But this statement still leaves the important question of what, in most cases, will prompt an AAG actually to overrule a positive recommendation in those cases where he does so.

These reasons, by and large, are drawn from the same category of questions that the trial lawyers themselves ask of their cases. The answers from the AAG's office, not surprisingly, are sometimes different, but the reasons do not represent the explicit injection of a new kind of consideration into the decision process. Even when the major issue at hand is a relatively large and policy-relevant one—for instance, when a new theory is emerging, as happened with the aggregate concentration argument in the conglomerate merger cases—it will be discussed in the AAG's office in much the same terms as those the staff lawyers themselves have already used in making their decisions: how good the argument is, whether it is likely to be persuasive, and whether the issue involved is important enough to warrant trying the theory even at a relatively large risk.

More rarely, these discussions do reveal more systematic splits between the AAG's office and the rest of the organization. One reported example concerned mergers in which an industry is dominated by one or more giant firms, and two nondominant but still-powerful firms wanted to merge in order to compete on a more nearly equal basis with the ruling giants. The question asked at both the staff level and the AAG level was whether the merger would decrease competition in the industry by eliminating a competitor or actually increase it by creating a more effective rival to the giants; from all reports, the AAG's office was somewhat more inclined to consider the possibility that the latter might be the case. But even with this example, the split was by no means an entirely clear one. Some of the trial lawyers who participated in this particular debate mentioned that when disputes like this occurred, there was usually a split in the staff itself; and even those who advocated cases against mergers of this type said that the dispute was a legitimate one, with both sides having persuasive arguments at their disposal. As one lawyer remembered his own discussions with the AAG in instances of this type, "It's nothing new, what he says. The same arguments take place all up and down the line."

Some differences between the AAG's office and the staff seem to be more systematic still, though it is difficult to confirm the information one gathers about them. For instance, the AAG's office has been said to have a particular sensitivity to the effect of Antitrust actions on the short-run performance of the economy in general and of the stock market in particular. For another, the office seemed to be specially solicitous of certain industries closely involved in national defense or with foreign governments. The staff lawyers tended to be highly skeptical when a defense matériel producer argued that a restrictive arrangement was necessary if its product was to continue being made under conditions favorable to the government; the AAG was said to be more sensitive both to the danger inherent in not taking such an argument seriously and to the probability that if *he* were not suitably sensitive, someone in the attorney general's office would doubtless be so.

Those two differences were said to have been apparent over the administrations of several recent assistant attorneys general. Other such differences are reported of only one AAG or another; most of these can only be described as idiosyncratic. Occasionally an AAG has refused to bring cases out of systematic beliefs on the subject of economics in general or on somewhat narrower topics such as unemployment. But more frequently mentioned were incidents such as that of a company president who personally convinced an AAG that his product was so beneficial that a proposed merger that would speed its development ought not to be challenged, or even of the AAG who was said to have turned down a case in the ladies' underwear industry simply because "he said he didn't want to be known as the man who brought the ladies' panties and girdles case."

Thus the AAG's office overrules for two broad kinds of reasons. There is the kind that the staff lawyers think wholly impermissible or seriously overvalued: the personal idiosyncrasies, or the belief that some other factor—short-run local employment, or the rapid development of a new product, or national defense—simply takes precedence over antitrust enforcement. But reasons of this sort seem to have influence only rarely; by and large, the AAG's office does not seem to operate from a set of standards very different from those of the trial lawyers or their section chiefs or the director of operations. More commonly, the AAG overrules for reasons that the lawyers recognize to be wholly within the framework of conventional antitrust enforcement itself, though the staff will of course object when the balance has been tipped against prosecution in their particular case.

It may be objected that this has been a perverse description of routine decisions in the division. It began with a full chapter devoted to the lowest-ranking members of the hierarchy, and it progressively shortened as it dealt with members who exercise progressively more formal authority. The reason for the progression, though, is that once one has described how the staff lawyers make their cases, one can best describe the process by which their superiors review them as a modification rather than by referring to any new and separate principles.

To say this is not to say an AAG's influence is small. He has perhaps his largest impact in the way subjects are initially chosen for investigation, and at the final stage he can, and sometimes does, simply overrule. Moreover, the modifications he more often makes are by no means trivial in determining the division's final product of filed cases. A case moves up the hierarchy as far as the director of operations' office facing an ever-increasing tension between the imperatives of prosecution and the demands of what superiors see as both the division's reputation for winning its cases and its reputation for legal craftsmanship in general. But the contrast between the two sets of criteria should not be overdrawn. The staff lawyers themselves value what they think of as a reputation for "solid" legal work and for winning the cases they bring. And those who are most rigorous in their criticism of weak cases believe that by their rigor they are in the long run strengthening the division's prosecutorial power. They fear the effect of too many acquittals on the number of cases the division will be able to bring successfully in the future, as well as on the business behavior that they think the division's reputation affects. In the usual situation, the two sets of standards do not seriously conflict. When they do, they seem not to do so systematically enough for the staff to be able, even if they were willing, to alter the great bulk of their work to suit the AAG's anticipated tastes or radically change the population of potential cases that he chooses from.

For most AAG's, this mode of procedure has seemed to pose no particular problems. But an organization like the division does pose serious potential problems for a chief executive who wants to impose on it some particular antitrust enforcement policy. For one thing, the combination of staff incentives to prosecute and the process of refinement through which cases pass before reaching the AAG's office should severely limit the chief executive's ability to stop cases he receives unless he is willing to risk damage to the organization's morale and to his own reputation. Conversely, it is hard to see how the chief executive can have many ways of systematically adding to the population of cases that come before him for approval. Recent AAGs have faced this problem and devised various strategies to mitigate it. The next chapter will examine these strategies, their varying degrees of success, and what they reveal about the division's distinctive capacities.

6
Functions of the Executive: Innovation

The great majority of cases in the Antitrust Division, and even most attempts to apply the antitrust laws in novel ways, originate with the staff lawyers. What usually happens to these cases and new ideas at the organization's higher levels may fairly be called a process of refinement, modification, and ratification. It is a process in which the assistant attorney general is only one of several authoritative voices, even though his formal power is of course the greatest. In most cases, in other words, the AAG does not play an architectonic role.

But the executive is not wholly without resources in this process, nor does he lack incentives to use them. As for reasons why an AAG may want to step up his activity, we have seen that sometimes they have consisted simply of strong personal views about the proper nature of antitrust enforcement in general. Sometimes an AAG has held narrower but just as strong opinions on more specific antitrust issues. Sometimes an AAG has taken his bearings from the views prevailing in the private antitrust bar. And sometimes, though less frequently, an AAG has wanted to change the division's product out of responsiveness, proper or improper, to pressures and direction from other parts of the federal government.

When an AAG does want to intervene in this way, he has the authority to step in at any of a number of stages. An AAG may intervene during the original dissemination of information to the staff, either on an ad hoc personal basis or by establishing new formal structures to encourage or discourage certain kinds of cases. In addition, an AAG may intervene, again personally or through formally established units, in the case review procedure, and again either to encourage or to discourage various cases and arguments. In recent years, AAGs have used all these techniques. This chapter asks how and under what circumstances such direction from the top has been successful in affecting the division's output.

Part of the explanation for an AAG's success or failure in these attempts lies with the opinions and responses of the staff. The foregoing chapters' description of the staff's goals and incentives suggests several predictions about how they will view executive attempts to intervene in or change their activities. First, one would expect many of these attempts they will either welcome or simply not care about one way or the other. If the executive suggests new arguments that would bring more cases within the division's reach or new prosecuting units that show reasonable promise of being able to reach new cases in special or esoteric areas, the staff, according to this prediction, will have no objection in principle. If a new prosecuting unit or function seriously infringes upon the commodity jurisdictions that the various sections have established, one would expect some resistance, both because the sections do not want to give up cases in these areas and because they think they already have the superior expertise. But if the effect on their own activities is marginal, or if they can be met by a strong argument that a new and specialized expertise can in fact bring about an increase in the division's overall activity, one might expect the resistance to be muted, at least in its public expression.

In the same way, one would expect that the staff attitude toward new arguments and theories presented to them would be determined by similar imperatives of prosecution. Of particular interest, since the role of economic reasoning in antitrust cases is so central and of such issue, the staff should show no antagonism in principle toward the theories or mode of reasoning created by academic economists. If the lawyers want to win cases, they should be willing to borrow any economic theory or a theory from any other discipline that works—that is, any theory that a federal court will accept as a basis for judging that a violation has been committed.

On the one hand, this purpose should make the lawyers theoretically adventurous. They are not constrained by academic conventions or fashions and so should have no qualms about adopting a theory that is controversial within the profession of economics but that in the lawyers' judgment appears to be a useful vehicle for enforcing the antitrust laws. On the other hand, the lawyers have one very conservative requirement for any economic theory they accept: They have to be able to find evidence to support it, evidence of the particular type that will appeal to noneconomist federal judges. In short, the lawyers' attitude toward economic argument should depend on which particular economic theories, tools, and predictions are under consideration and how well these contributions from economics meet their prosecutorial needs.

Finally, this same analysis of the lawyers' goals provides predictions about what structural organizational changes they will resent and strongly resist. First, they will oppose any change that they see as implying that they can bring fewer cases—any change that restricts in advance the population of cases from which they can choose or the arguments they can use. Second, we should find them opposing any change that implies to them a general disrespect for their professional judgment or for the criteria they use to make their decisions.

Bearing these predictions in mind, one may examine a representative sample of major changes that recent AAGs have tried to make in the organization. The following list is by no means exhaustive; its examples are chosen precisely to cast light on the predictions above. But the examples that have been excluded do not give a different lesson from those that have been included. It should further be borne in mind that the list's purpose is not to include or exclude items according to whether they in fact constitute "true innovations" according to some rigorous definition of the term. Anything mentioned by staff or executive as innovative has been accepted as such, because the purpose here is to examine executives' success at imposing what they see to be their agenda and to examine staff reactions to what they themselves see as impinging on their mode of work.

New Functional Units

Assistant attorneys general seem to have considerable leeway in establishing new units to do specialized antitrust jobs. AAGs have not attempted any general reorganization of the division that would wholly replace the "commodity" basis around which a good deal of the division's work is now structured. But there is little effective resistance to functional organization in more specific areas that the staff recognizes as discrete and limited.

One major change of this type has been the expansion of the division's activities in the regulated industries. The change began as early as 1961, when then–Assistant Attorney General Lee Loevinger decided that all of the division's transportation-industry work should be gathered into one section. Those who participated in the change knew that they were not merely regrouping similar commodities but establishing a new, specialized functional expertise as well: The transportation industries not only had certain internal features in common but were also in large part regulated, so their treatment would presumably benefit from both an increased commodity expertise among the lawyers who handled them and a special expertise in dealing with regulatory agencies.

Still, the AAG thought of the change as a "technical" one, a "tidying up," and insofar as he had larger purposes in mind, the goal of affecting regulation was only an indistinct part of a larger and even less sharply defined goal. It is true that when the section was reorganized, it was formed so that it could in the future reach out beyond the transportation industry itself: The AAG did expand the section's size rather than merely taking transportation lawyers from existing sections, and the additional lawyers, it seems, were to establish a capacity to do something more than transportation cases. "I didn't want it just specifically for the regulated sector," Loevinger remembered about the new section. "I wanted a broad section, with consumer functions. I wanted it to be able to deal with *any* agency or legislative body and present the consumer viewpoint." So Loevinger had at least two things in mind: a possible expansion of transportation activity through an increase in commodity and regulatory expertise and an increase in certain types of nonprosecutorial work, even apart from intervention in regulatory agency proceedings.

This was also the way the staff and the existing section chiefs saw it, and they did not much object. "There wasn't much jurisdictional fuss," Loevinger remembered, and others agree:

The other section chiefs thought this was a sideline to their basic activities. They're oriented to the federal courts—whereas in this section now, half our work is done with the agencies. Most of them had never done agency work, and each of them saw this field as just a little piece of their action. They were happy to be free to concentrate on other things.

So this particular change in jurisdiction caused no great disagreement because other lawyers recognized that a special expertise was involved, considered agency activities not only marginal to their own but not even "prosecution" in the full sense of practice in the courts, and certainly had no quarrel with someone else's undertaking those broader consumer-advocacy functions which were even more clearly nonprosecutorial in nature.

Subsequent AAGs continued to expand the section—it is now roughly as big as any regular prosecuting section—and in the mid-1960s, "things really began to get rolling," as one present public counsel section member recalled. "We finally got an adequate staff," one member explained. And another of the section's lawyers, who arrived in 1965, argued more specifically that it was he who "finally put this section on the map."

He went on to tell what he meant by "putting this section on the map": "Why, this section brings almost as many cases in the federal courts now as any of the regular prosecuting sections." Another attorney in the public counsel section added, "It used to be that they didn't even call us trial lawyers. We didn't even get the trial lawyers' manual." "But," he added proudly, "that's all changed now."

It is true that the founding of this new section marked—though it was not consciously noted at the time—the beginning of a certain diversification of the division's functions, a somewhat increasing attention by the organization as a whole to the uses of not only interventions but legislation and intragovernmental consultation as vehicles for spreading antitrust and procompetitive doctrines. And the public counsel section does continue to participate in these newer organizational activities. But what strikes the observer is not the fact of this participation but that, despite it, this section's lawyers have come to think of themselves not as general consumer advocates, as ready to use forums in the executive as outside it, but as something not unlike the prosecuting attorneys to be found in "regular" sections. A good part of the public counsel staff shared the view of the young man who said of the work he was sometimes assigned to do, commenting on various congressional bills that would affect the division, "That stuff's a pain. I wouldn't really mind working on something big—like the deregulation of the _____ industry that _____ is doing. . . . " He went on to say that under normal circumstances, the kind of work he liked best was work in the federal courts.

The lawyers in the public counsel section continually face two problems that the other staff lawyers do not have. One is that when they deal with regulatory agencies rather than federal courts, they have a less sympathetic audience for arguments about the importance of antitrust doctrine. The agencies, to speak very generally, need not disallow a business practice or action simply because it would violate antitrust law in an unregulated industry, and many practices that have long been considered violations of antitrust law by the courts still need to be proved undesirable before the agencies. "Hell," one public counsel lawyer said, "we're still trying to establish doctrines at the _____ Commission that have been antitrust law for twenty years." The second persistent problem is a more technical one: When the division wants to take a regulated company to court, it often must deal with the question of whether a regulatory agency's jurisdiction over the company protects it from prosecution.

But neither of these differences has much effect on the public counsel lawyers' view of antitrust's proper role, on their basic information-gathering and investigating procedures, on their standards of evidence, or on their criteria for deciding what a good case or an anticompetitive practice is. The public counsel section operates with regard to particular cases much as the other sections do, aside from the special constraint imposed by what it sees as some regulatory agencies' benighted views; the general description of the Antitrust staff lawyers fits these Antitrust lawyers as well.

To sum up, the establishment of the public counsel section was a relatively noncontroversial action because at the time it took little away from existing sections in terms of available cases and posed no challenge to existing criteria for the selection of antitrust cases in general. Insofar as the section has fulfilled its original aims, it has done so mainly by extending the organization's existing principles and criteria to new areas. Insofar as it has departed from the original aims, it has done so by becoming more strongly prosecution-oriented, more involved with the federal courts, and more like the division of which it is a part.

A similar sequence of opinions and events marked the founding of the division's patents unit. In the late 1960s, under the administration of Assistant Attorney General Donald Turner, a special team was organized in the evaluations section to investigate ways in which existing patent law could be made more compatible with antitrust principles. But the decision actually to establish a permanent patents unit, with operating responsibilities and routine jurisdiction over patents cases, was made shortly after Richard McLaren took office as assistant attorney general in 1969. McLaren's reasons for establishing the patents unit sound similar to those Loevinger gave for establishing the public counsel section: "It was just pulling together in one office all the lawyers with patent and technical training. We just consolidated the work there. This was just technical." McLaren added a further comment: "It wasn't particularly to step up activity in the area; it wasn't to break new ground in the patent field."

On the other hand, others involved in the unit's founding did want to expand division work in the patents area and did have certain rulings they wanted to overturn. The man McLaren chose to head the new patents unit was by career and temperament an aggressive prosecutor and had been a member of Turner's original exploratory patents task force. So if McLaren had no expansionary aims of his own in mind, at least there is no evidence that he was averse to such aims in others.

Once again, there was little resistance from the section chiefs who were about to lose jurisdiction over certain cases. One man involved in this founding remembered, "There weren't many objections from the chiefs. Only one of them had any serious interest in the area at all." There was resistance from some men in the front office. These men had no personal jurisdictional interest in the outcome; they simply argued that commodity expertise in these cases was more important than patents expertise. But by all accounts, it was not the section chiefs who formed the major source of opposition: As with the regulated industries, patents were seen as very technical and as marginal to the regular sections' activities.

And, like the public counsel section, like all the special sections of the division, the patents unit bears the marks of the special circumstances under which it was founded and so is in some ways distinct from the regular prosecuting sections. One difference lies simply in the special backgrounds and expertise of some of its members; several of them have studied engineering or, because the new section wanted a rapid infusion of expertise, were private patent lawyers before joining the division. Further, as with the regulated industries, the status of antitrust doctrine in the field of patents law is considered "backward." Many restrictive practices long prohibited by the courts for business in general are permitted where the article under consideration is patented.

Partly because of this perceived "backwardness," the patent lawyers in the division are especially aware of the existence of new ground to break. They seem to have a common and specific list of goals, all of them desired constraints on a patentee's power to engage in practices that would otherwise be illegal under the antitrust laws. "I guess we *do* know what to do," one of them remarked. "For instance, sooner or later we're going to overrule the _____ decision."

In this sense the patents unit lawyers are more programmatic than their colleagues. They are not so interested in picking up any existing violation as they are in overruling certain offensive doctrines in the patents field. But this programmatic cast of mind is the result of the particular state of antitrust law with regard to patents rather than of any difference between them and other division lawyers on what does or should constitute an antitrust violation or on how to go about establishing one. And it by no means excludes completely their prosecution of cases that come their way and that simply involve a large amount of commerce or an egregiously clear violation of existing law.

So the patents unit was also a noncontroversial change. It involved the extension of agreed-on antitrust principles to a new area; it threatened very little the goals, methods of operation, or available cases in the existing sections; and it proved not to be a difficult or organizationally costly undertaking for an executive. The new patents unit began with a more programmatic cast of mind than one sees in the older, less specialized prosecuting sections. But this difference cannot be said to constitute evidence of a prevailing ethos that is fundamentally different from that of the rest of the division.

Antitrust "Campaigns"

The list of structural changes that have taken place in the division at various times could be extended at length. Complaints sections have been established and abolished, a merger section founded and done away with, judgment and enforcement sections split and recombined, a consumer protection group and an oil industry group added, new functions assigned to various parts of the policy planning staff. The very frequency of such changes is a clue that they entail relatively low organizational costs.

But staff lawyers are also amenable, in general, to another kind of intervention by the AAG in the division's workings: the initiation of "campaigns" against particular offenses or industries and the encouragement of particular cases or theories within the division. This kind of activity by AAGs is at least as old as the administration of Thurman Arnold. One recent example of this type was the decision by a then–assistant attorney general to mount a campaign against the practice of reciprocity—agreement between two companies to give each other preferential treatment in their purchases. The practice had already been disapproved by the courts under some circumstances.[1] But, as Assistant Attorney General Richard McLaren remembered, "I saw it happening when I was in private practice, so I had it in mind when I came to the division. It was illegal, but when I was in private practice, I'd never been able to sell the government on moving on these things. When I came, I got things moving quickly."

There is no doubt that things did get "moving quickly," and with no great difficulty. Within a year, several reciprocity cases had been prepared against manufacturing companies in basic industries.[2] This ease and speed seem to have stemmed from two causes. First, not only the new AAG but the staff as well saw the offense as a relatively clear one. Second, several cases on the issue were already in various stages of investigation when the directive to move came from the AAG. What McLaren says he did to speed these cases, and what the staff lawyers report the front office did, was simply to tell the director of operations to direct the lawyers to give special attention to the pending investigations and to offer suggestions, from personal experience, of other companies to be investigated.

Staff lawyers who worked on these investigations certainly report no resentment at having their energies redirected in this way.

To the contrary, they expressed overwhelming approval of what the AAG had done. From their point of view, these cases were clear, good, and winnable. Further, such cases developed the additional virtue of being very likely to receive quick and favorable attention from the front office. In other words, the staff is by no means opposed to executive direction if it is exercised in behalf of the staff's own notions of good antitrust prosecution.

Even when an AAG tries to implement such a campaign by partially supplanting the division's traditional methods of gathering information, the staff is at least tolerant and sometimes favorable. For example, the division's economics section was at one point directed to survey the prices of selected commodities in various cities—to look for an unusually high and inflexible price for a commodity in a given city, or suspicious parallelism in price changes by different firms, and report it to the appropriate prosecuting section or field office as a clue that firms might be fixing the price of that commodity.

Those lawyers who received information from this price survey did reveal some skepticism about the usefulness of this new technique of information gathering, simply because it does not provide one with any direct evidence that a price-fix has in fact taken place. As one of them put it, "The _____ industry is *loaded* with price-fixing. . . . I know that industry is loaded with price-fixing. But that's not evidence; you have to get someone to squeal." But this suspicion was by no means active opposition, nor did it imply any special reluctance to use the data that the surveys provided when these data could be used to support other, independently gathered evidence in an industry the lawyer was already investigating or already suspicious of. Most of the lawyers asked about the price survey gave some version of the following judgment by one of them: "Yeah, it's been okay. We've gotten a couple of cases out of it." In short, the staff seemed not unhappy to absorb new kinds of information that could help them bring more cases of the type they considered acceptable.

Intervention by the front office need not concern already clear offenses in order for staff lawyers to consider it acceptable or even desirable. The staff is by no means averse to adopting new theories or arguments from the front office where such changes give them a chance to bring a case they might not have been able to bring otherwise. As in the case of decisions to concentrate on a special offense, it is often hard to tell exactly where in the division these new theories originate. But even if a possible new argument has long been discussed by the staff, the front office nevertheless seems sometimes to have played a crucial role in deciding whether a particular novel idea was to be used in a particular case at hand.

One example of such a departure is provided by the story of the "potential competition" theory. Because of the special provisions of the 1960 Bank Mergers Act,[3] the division must be asked its opinion of any proposed bank merger and given the opportunity to announce its intention to oppose a merger. This requirement has given the division an unusually full and systematic source of information on mergers in this field. After several years of dealing with bank mergers under the new law, one division banking lawyer reported, "We just didn't *get* merger proposals any more where the banks were actually in direct competition." The typical problem, from the point of view of division lawyers, became a proposed merger in which two banks were not in direct competition. Typically, a bank in a certain state would want to buy an independent bank in some town at the other end of the state where the first bank did not have an office or perform any services. What worried the division lawyers about these proposals was the removal of possible future independent entrants from the markets in which these acquisitions were taking place; if a bank could buy an already existing facility in another town, it had little incentive to establish a competing facility of its own.

One way to argue against allowing such a merger, as the lawyers involved remembered their experience, was to contend that if the acquiring bank were prohibited from making its acquisition in the new market, it would indeed probably enter the new market on its own, thus adding to the number of independent competitors in the area. This was a fairly well-established argument,[4] and one that the division did use in bank merger cases. But from the division's point of view, it had a significant drawback. To prove to a judge's satisfaction that the acquiring bank would "probably" enter the new market on its own if it were not allowed to merge, the prosecution had to present some kind of evidence—from the bank's internal communications or its past record of behavior—that the bank might in fact have considered such an independent move and might have been capable of making it. These attempts by the division could easily prove unsuccessful, either because the required evidence did not exist or because the bank could produce strong counterevidence—for instance, a statement by a state banking official that he would not *permit* internal expansion of this type. Such counterarguments could seriously weaken any case based on the idea of "probable entry."[5]

So a decision was made in the division not to continue to rely exclusively on "probable entry" arguments but at least to supplement them with arguments about "potential entry," or "potential competition."[6] The "potential competition" argument was similar to an argument about "probable entry," but the two differed in an important way. Like "probable entry," the "potential competition" argument contends that a merger may be harmful because it removes possible future independent competitors. But "potential competition" is an economist's notion, not a lawyer's. It requires less evidence of the acquiring company's past actions or expressions of intent. It requires only that the company and market at issue show certain "objective" characteristics—of size, expertise, barriers to entry, rate of market growth, market structure, and such—that make the market theoretically attractive and the company theoretically capable of entry. In other words, this more radical version of the argument removes from a prosecutor much of the need to support his case with what the lawyers call "subjective" evidence about companies' past conduct.

The decision that the division should begin to rely on this "potential competition" version of the argument came, as one staff lawyer involved reported, "from the top—from the front office. It was a combination of the front office wanting to use this theory and the staff itself trying to get a handle on a difficult case." It is true that there was never anything like a staff consensus on whether or not this new theory should be used. "There were constant squabbles over it," one front office man remembered. And a staff lawyer recalled, "Until the day before the trial in [one] case, we were discussing the theory." Yet another staff lawyer remembered, "It's true that there was a certain reluctance about accepting this. It's weird to have to use a theory without any evidence." On the other hand, the decision by the front office was far from being a simple imposition of doctrine against the lawyers' will. "It certainly wasn't just shoved down our throats," one lawyer remembered. "We had been discussing it ourselves, and we certainly saw the virtue of it too."

The staff was, on balance, inclined to accept the judgment of the front office because, as one lawyer said, "We couldn't have won on 'probability' anyway." In other words, the staff ultimately agreed that the argument should be used because it brought a set of cases within their reach. But several among them were more than a little skeptical about whether the argument would actually work in court.

The division did not do well in court with its "potential competition" theory.[7] Even staff lawyers who ultimately abandoned their resistance to its use or felt no special resentment toward it in the first place took some intellectual satisfaction from its failure. Such satisfaction was apparent in a story that almost every division lawyer involved in the banking cases—and many who were not— seemed to want to tell about what the judge had said to the division lawyer who had tried one particular "potential competition" case. "The judge peered over the bench," one typical version of the story went, "and he said to _____, 'You've given me probabilities and potentialities and possibilities and theories—but no *evidence*.'"

The staff was willing to try the new argument because it gave them a chance to win cases they thought they could not have won otherwise. But they were confirmed in some of their basic opinions when this approach to antitrust enforcement from economic theory did not work in court. They did not mind having their suspicion borne out that the tools and methods with which they are most familiar are, at least in the short run, the tools and methods of the most effective enforcement. One of them summed up his experience with the "potential competition" theory by saying, "Maybe the industry is just too complicated for the theory. After all, there's nothing wrong with the theory, but antitrust law is still based on *facts*."

More briefly, the same pattern of tolerance and skepticism is revealed in the fate of another recent attempt to introduce a new argument into the division's arsenal: the "aggregate concentration" theory. The largest of the conglomerate mergers that took place in the 1960s had long worried division staff lawyers—because of the tendency of conglomerates to buy leading firms in the various industries they entered rather than adding their resources to smaller firms, because of the increased potential these mergers created for specific anticompetitive practices, and most of all because of the sheer size of the acquiring companies. The staff had been prevented from filing some cases against such mergers in these years because of opinion in the front office that the law as it stood simply could not be applied to such cases. When a new AAG took office in 1969, he announced that he would begin a campaign of vigorous prosecution of these conglomerate mergers, and, as in the case of the reciprocity campaign, the proposed complaints did emerge from the division staff.

But from the division's point of view, the arguments upon which the trial lawyers proposed to base their cases were in some respects weak. These weaknesses were analogous to those the division had found in the "probable entry" bank arguments. For instance, the existence of a conglomerate structure presumably gives the member companies increased opportunities for practices such as reciprocity. But it may not be possible to show from a conglomerate's past behavior that it is in fact likely to use its corporate resources to engage in such practices. Or, to take another example, purchase by a rich conglomerate of a powerful firm might be thought to "entrench" the purchased firm in its position of market power through various applications of the corporate resources. But it may not be possible to show from the parent firm's past record that it is in fact likely to use its resources for such entrenchment or that such use would have much effect on the overall competitive situation in the industry in question. Moreover, the anticonglomerate arguments of this period were systematically weaker than conventional antimerger arguments for the simple reason that "pure" conglomerates, by definition, do not make their acquisitions in those lines of commerce in which they are already engaged. Many people expressed doubt, therefore, about whether the Clayton Act prohibition against mergers likely to lessen competition "in any line of commerce" applied to these mergers.

The staff saw these as the weaknesses of the arguments readily available to them, and they were aware of another theory on the undesirability of conglomerate mergers: the "aggregate concentration" theory.[8] Briefly, it argued that the economy as a whole could properly be considered a "line of commerce" just as its component parts could, and that an increase of concentration in the economy as a whole would have anticompetitive effects like those the courts had already accepted as following from the increase in concentration within one particular market.

As with the "potential competition" argument, the "aggregate concentration" theory had a great virtue from the staff's point of view: It reduced their reliance on a whole category of problematic evidence, in this case evidence of specific anticompetitive effects in particular lines of commerce. In theory, it thus brought a new class of cases more easily within the division's reach. But again like the "potential competition" theory, "aggregate concentration" had a serious drawback. Precisely because it was so independent of specific evidence of a merger's probable effect in any one market, it was not thought that it would be attractive to a court.

The staff had been discussing the theory before the front office encouraged them to use it in court, and as one front office member recalls it, "We had an easier time getting them to accept this one than we did with potential competition." On the other hand, if the staff members revealed no resistance to the theory, neither does it seem that they expressed any great enthusiasm for it. Almost every lawyer interviewed on the subject gave some variation of the following comment: "I never did understand that theory in the first place. And I don't think anyone else around here did, either." A few even expressed some satisfaction that in motions for preliminary injunctions, testimony about the theory had not even been admitted into evidence.[9] In sum, once again the staff accepted the theory because it gave them additional ammunition in cases where they admitted many of their more conventional arguments were weak; but they embraced it only reluctantly, and certainly reserved judgment on it, because it failed to meet what they considered important requirements for any successful antitrust argument.

One may say more generally that the staff has proved willing to exploit new arguments suggested by the front office when they present some hope of "getting a handle" on a preexisting difficult case or set of cases. In the absence of a preexisting case—as with results from the economics section's price surveys—they will use new information as an adjunct to the information they can gather through more traditional methods. But when a new theory or argument emerges from the front office and neither deals with a clear offense nor meets the lawyers' needs in a specific case, it is not likely to be pursued by the staff. Or at least that is the implication to be drawn from the fate of the "shared monopoly" theory.

This argument was proposed by parts of the front office during the administration of Assistant Attorney General Donald Turner, who took office in 1965 and served until 1968. It contended that in some oligopolistic industries, the conduct of the ruling giants was so closely parallel and so clearly mutually protective, the barrier to entry and the profits so high, as to amount to evidence of joint monopolization; this pattern, therefore, was liable to prosecution under the Sherman Act. The theory was disseminated in the form of a memo from the front office to the prosecuting sections; the memo identified a number of industries whose conduct was such as to make the theory an accurate and persuasive description.

Now there were limits on the resources devoted to the introduction of this new theory as a basis for beginning investigations by the trial staff. The pressure of other business prevented the AAG from devoting sustained attention to it, and the theory as presented then was by no means so well developed as it later became.[10] But at the level below the assistant attorney general, the policy planning staff did meet with various trial lawyers in an effort to encourage "shared monopoly" cases. In time the policy planners abandoned this effort because cases of this type simply were not brought forward by the trial staff and indeed because trial lawyers and section chiefs were quite explicit in telling them why the cases were not appearing. The staff lawyers acquainted with the industries in question simply never reported their industries as appropriate candidates for a court test of the idea. People who were members of the evaluations section at the time, and who spoke to the trial lawyers about this absence of response, said later that the trial lawyers were probably right: "They *showed* us 'radicals' why we couldn't do it, even though they were *anxious* to bring these cases." One of the trial lawyers involved summarized succinctly what the problem with the theory was, from the point of view of a courtroom lawyer: "I wouldn't want to try a case on that theory—I think it stinks. You're trying to prove intent, but you have no *evidence*. They just react to each other—*necessarily*. The whole area is spooky."

In short, there was no preexisting case whose circumstances seemed clearly to resemble those envisioned by the theory, no ongoing or past investigations that had unearthed what the lawyers considered suitable evidence of the quasi-conspiratorial conduct. The theory was attractive, the trial lawyers thought, but of little help in gathering the evidence necessary to make a case.

The foregoing description of the fate of some new theories suggests that the cirteria for their acceptance by the division staff are fairly simple. If the front office intervenes to encourage cases involving what the lawyers think of as clear offenses, the intervention will be welcomed. If it provides information to supplement the lawyers' own, it will be willingly accepted. If the front office encourages a new theory to mitigate the problems that the staff lawyers meet in ongoing investigations, the staff might be skeptical of the extent to which such an argument will "work" in court but will probably withhold judgment of the theory, subject to the test of actual courtroom experience. If the executive supplies a new theory that does *not* speak specifically to the needs of cases closely at hand, the lawyers will not spend much time looking for cases to fit the theory. In sum, staff attitudes toward direction by their superiors are determined by their own needs as prosecutors eager to bring more cases but conservative in their perceptions of what kinds of evidence they need in order to win these cases, prosecutors prone to focus their attention on the cases immediately before them.

Staff Veto

So far, the staff has been described as fairly tolerant of direction by the executive. It must be remembered, though, that the direction described so far has been of the type that attempts to expand the number of cases within the division's reach or is at least not inimical to that expansion. When the effect of such direction is the opposite—when it is seen to limit this field of available cases—the staff has not proved so tolerant.

Such attempts have not occurred often; by far the majority of recent AAGs have not had much in the way of systematic antitrust preferences or policies that excluded some types of cases as well as encouraging others. It is therefore illuminating to examine the case of one AAG who did have such.

Assistant Attorney General Donald Turner had an antitrust background that was particularly distinguished. Most of his recent predecessors had been practicing lawyers at the time of their appointments, and their schooling after college had been exclusively in the law. Turner, by contrast, had gained a Ph.D. in economics before entering law school, and he was at the time of his appointment a professor at Harvard Law School, where he was widely acknowledged as one of the country's chief authorities on American antitrust law. His recent predecessors in office had allowed the organization to maintain itself, had exercised only sporadically their power of reversal through ultimate review, and had tried to leave their mark on the organization in the form of major cases tried, particular extensions of the law in doctrine, campaigns against particular offenses or industries, reorganizations to foster certain kinds of special expertise, or expansions of division activity into previously untouched fields.

Assistant Attorney General Turner, at the time of his appointment, had a somewhat clearer and more ambitious goal. He was concerned not only about the division's expansion into new areas but also about what he considered the declining quality of the division's work product. The decline in the work, as he saw it, had been of two sorts. First, recent Supreme Court decisions had been so favorable to the division and so imprecise in their prescriptions that the lawyers were developing overconfidence and a sloppiness in the purely legal aspects of their arguments, as well as a certain lack of rigor in their thinking about the purposes for which they were bringing cases. Second, the division proceeded largely in ignorance that its task, as Turner understood it, was essentially economic and that its tools, its ordering of goals, and its arguments must therefore be those of good economics. The division, in Turner's view, was bringing too many cases of small economic importance; it was bringing too many cases on the basis of bad economic theory and bad economic analysis. "Things were really sloppy over there," one of Turner's staffers remembers of his arrival. "The lawyers were recommending that we prosecute mergers because the mergers would make the new company more efficient, and all the other guys would get driven out." It would not be accurate simply to say that Turner went to the division wanting to replace the existing legal criteria for decisions with the standards of economics. Instead, he saw in the existing division important failings both of economics and of law.

Turner had few illusions about the difficulty of making the improvements he had in mind. He was familiar with the division's routines and its decision rules, and he never assumed that he could undertake a wholesale revision of them on every level. Instead, he proceeded in a way that seemed reasonable in light of his goals: He established new structures, staffed them with new personnel, and promulgated written guides to constrain the lawyers' decisions and to limit the effects of those decisions.

Turner's major structural innovations were the evaluations section and the larger policy planning unit of which it was a part. An evaluations section had in fact been established by Turner's predecessor, but at the time of Turner's appointment, it included three people and is said to have had little effect on the division's activities. Turner expanded the evaluations section to fifteen people and gave it formal responsibility for reviewing every proposed case after it left the office of the director of operations and before it came to the AAG's office. In its review, the evaluations section was supposed to clarify the theory of proposed cases—eliminating, if necessary, evidence that might possibly be helpful in winning a case but that would obscure the legal point for which the case was to be brought; to make sure that cases were not brought on the basis of bad economic arguments or for bad economic purposes; and to discourage the filing of cases that were neither economically nor legally important enough to warrant the use of the division's limited resources.

The section also had the potential function of helping the trial lawyers "save" cases that might otherwise have been unacceptable, by finding new theories and even assisting the trial lawyers in finding new evidence of the applicability of these theories. Many trial lawyers did in fact benefit from this use of the section, but it is not a benefit that they afterward considered to have been important or, indeed, that they often recalled on their own.

Turner also tried to bring some more order to the division's merger prosecutions. In the interests of equity and to ensure that the division would concentrate its energies on economically important mergers, he directed the publication of a set of merger guidelines, for the use of both division lawyers and outside defense counsel. The guidelines, when they finally appeared, listed in unprecedented detail the objective economic-structural conditions that would make a merger presumptively objectionable in the division's eyes.[11] For instance, one provision read:

7. *Market with Trend Toward Concentration.* The Department applies an additional, stricter standard in determining whether to challenge mergers occurring in any market, not wholly unconcentrated, in which there is a significant trend toward increased concentration. Such a trend is considered to be present when the aggregate market share of any grouping of the largest firms in the market from the two largest to the eight largest has increased by approximately seven per cent or more of the market over a period of time extending from any base year 5–10 years prior to the merger. . . .

In addition to expanding the evaluations section and publishing the merger guidelines late in his administration, Turner took another step to improve the legal and economic quality of the division's product. He intervened personally and much more extensively in the review process than his predecessors had. He reviewed cases in much greater detail, and he made known both the types of cases he would not bring and the Supreme Court decisions he considered too broad and vague to be taken as a guide, in themselves, to division prosecutions. As he later summarized his attitude, "I didn't want the division to bring every case we *could* win. I wanted us to bring only the cases we *should* win."

Lawyers who were in the division at the time talked of Turner in terms much more resentful than those they used for the front office in general. In particular, almost every lawyer who was in the division during these years, when asked about them, seemed to have his own story of indignities suffered at the hands of the evaluations section, the AAG's personal staff, or the AAG himself. The most general complaint was about the simple delays that arose from the existence of "another level of bureaucracy." But this comment was usually only a preface to, and a mask for, complaints of another kind. That is, the organization has always been complained of as bureaucratic, but the Turner bureaucracy provoked a special indignation. One lawyer told that he had been working on a merger that did not meet the Clayton Act standards by eliminating a "substantial" amount of competition. But he thought he had found a way to attack the merger successfully through the Sherman Act:

The rule as I read it was simple. The merger of two large companies, eliminating just a *large* amount of competition, was illegal. . . . A certain Harvard professor was *shocked* at how the law had developed—because things were easier to prove under Section 1 of the Sherman Act than they were meant to be. He *raved* about this; he said you shouldn't be allowed to bring these merger cases under the easier standard of Section 1, otherwise, he said, there was no reason for two statutes. . . . He was persuaded . . . that there was this metaphysical distinction between the Sherman Act and the Clayton Act. . . . There was *always* this fundamental conflict—and he brought it to everyone's attention.

It was, to say the least, understandable that the lawyer's theory had been turned down, but the reasons accompanying the rejection obviously rankled.

Another lawyer remembered that in one case,

. . . they wanted to overrule the _____ doctrine. So we were ordered to bring the case *squarely* on _____. We had other kinds of evidence—but we never put it in. When it was time to appeal, McLaren was in. He was furious that we had left out evidence; he was a trial lawyer, and he knew you don't go halfway on cases. So we weren't going to bring cases any more just to establish a point of law; we were going to bring them to *win*. That was a big boost to morale.

Still another lawyer told of the time that the evaluations section had tried to discourage him from bringing a case: "_____ kept telling me that it was too small for me, that I was too valuable to waste on things like that. But it was a really nasty violation. I finally got it filed—I think it may not have been till McLaren came in."

As these stories reveal, the lawyers' dislike for the evaluations section and for the attitude that it embodied had several causes. It was not simply that the lawyers resented being reviewed at all; as was described in the last chapter, they are now and had previously been subject to several levels of review. But this time someone had, in the lawyers' eyes, changed the criteria of review, adding standards alien to the lawyers and repugnant to their notions of good prosecution. One did not turn down a case involving a clear, predatory violation of the law simply because it had little economic impact; one did not risk losing a case merely because winning it would require slight obfuscation of the case's most important legal aspect.

Similar reasoning lay behind the lawyers' opinions of the merger guidelines. The guidelines, as Turner was aware, were in some cases more conservative than current Supreme Court doctrine in defining the field of prosecutions open to the division. Moreover, they relied almost exclusively on economic-structural data, and they lent an unprecedented predictability to the division's actions in the merger field. All these factors led many of the staff to oppose the whole idea of guidelines; they did not want the division's discretion limited by this extralegal means. A veteran trial lawyer gave the following account of his attitude: "I can't remember any attempt to really set policy around here, except for Turner's guidelines. But this can only work against us. We're bound by the policy; the defendant's not. Fortunately, the courts have ruled that they're not the law. This kind of thing only says what the *incumbent's* policy is."

The changes that the Turner administration made had good as well as bad effects from the point of view of increasing the number of the division's cases, both in the short run and in the long run. The evaluations section did "save" cases as well as kill them. Also, the section was used not only for review but also to launch the division into new areas and into areas—such as intervention into regulatory proceedings—where the organization had begun to work but where its efforts were thought to deserve even more expansion.[12] Moreover, a decision to bring a case squarely on an attempt to overrule a certain precedent is an obvious investment in future division cases that would fall under the precedent. And finally, merger guidelines can be an aid as well as a bar to prosecution; they can encourage lawyers to investigate mergers that might not appear otherwise suspicious.

But staff lawyers, by and large, did not adopt any such balanced attitude toward this set of innovations. Just as we have seen that they tend to be tolerant when a doubtful argument expands their prosecutorial reach in the short run, they do not display much gratitude for possible long-term benefits when an intervention by the executive contracts their short-run, immediate reach.

Their attitude had its effect on the division when administrations changed. "The resentment had been building up for a long time," one Turner planner remembered, "before McLaren came in." And largely as a result of these opinions, within the division and in the antitrust bar to which the division is so closely connected, most of the changes that the staff found unacceptable were reversed. Cases were filed, such as anticonglomerate cases, that had been barred for economic policy reasons; the AAG assumed a smaller role in the case review process and did not argue so insistently that the staff tailor its presentation of evidence exclusively to the most important legal point to be made in a given case. The merger guidelines were no longer considered to be binding; lawyers asked about them said that they used the guidelines to call to their attention possible anticompetitive situations that they might not otherwise have seen, but they would not consider themselves barred from prosecuting mergers that were "legal" under the guidelines.

Moreover, the functions of the evaluations section and the policy planning staff of which it was a part changed. It kept and even expanded some of the functions it had previously held, undertaking even more prosecutions of its own and more interventions of all kinds in special areas newly important to the division or of special interest to the AAG or the director of policy planning.[13] But it no longer reviewed every proposed case. It could comment on any case it wished but was specifically asked to comment only on cases of special theoretical interest. In short, evaluations became less an organ of self-criticism and of the intrusion into ordinary cases of the front office's systematic policies and more of an advance-guard prosecuting section.

The division executive, then, has broad latitude in directing the division's course. An AAG may add new structures to institutionalize various special prosecutorial goals he wants the division to pursue, he may suggest and encourage cases of various types, and he can persuade the staff to adopt new arguments and theories that meet the needs of special cases. He may be able to promote new types of cases in the absence of specific information by assigning the task to a special elite section, but it is unlikely that he will be able to do so through the regular trial sections. And beyond his own tenure, it is unlikely that he can persuade a division of the present makeup and competences to adopt changes that limit its prosecutorial reach any more than that reach is limited by the courts.

7
External Influences

So far, the Antitrust Division's cases have been described as the product of the staff's desire to prosecute, some constraints of legal craftsmanship, and, to a lesser extent, the personal agenda of various assistant attorneys general. But there are other obvious places to look for determinations of that product. For one thing, the division is part of the Department of Justice and thus of the executive branch. Not only does it depend on the department, the Office of Management and Budget, and ultimately the White House for its money, it is also formally bound to take certain kinds of policy direction from the president.

Second, like other agencies, it also depends upon Congress for its budget and is subject to congressional oversight. And because the division initiates most of its actions in response to private complaints, it might be expected to feel considerable pressure from individual congressmen acting in behalf of constituents. Finally, the division's field of activity falls within the professional orbit of a highly coherent group of law specialists, the private antitrust bar. Precisely because the division performs a highly specialized professional task, it might be thought subject to special scrutiny by this attentive public.

Each of these groups might be thought to have more than sufficient reason to make use of its potential influence. On the one hand, the general idea of antitrust enforcement is a widely popular one. Therefore, scrutiny of the division in behalf of this consensual attitude should be a profitable stance for an elected official to take. On the other hand, most of the time the actions of the division are not highly visible to the general public, though they remain a subject of great interest to those businessmen and lawyers whose fortunes the division can affect. This situation of obscurity is said to have been a major factor in producing the classic clientalist pattern in which the immediately affected client group gains disproportionate influence over agency decisions. One might reasonably expect to find in the Antitrust Division this same pattern of private influence on particular cases.

In short, because of widespread approval for general antitrust goals and the relative obscurity of particular cases, one might suppose the division to be a frequent target for attempts at direction and influence by outside parties. The question is, do such efforts actually take place, and what effect do they have on the division's operations?

The Budget

One of the most obvious ways an administration or Congress might be expected to direct the division's overall level of activity and its allocation of resources is by controlling the organization's budget. And, in fact, some such control does exist. Yet the power of the purse seems rarely to be used to shape division policies or decisions about resource allocation. Each year the division draws up a budget request that asks for an increase in its appropriations. It is an increase that, by the time it emerges from the Office of Management and Budget, is a relatively small one: The request has reached eight hundred thousand dollars only four times in the past fifteen years. But what is more important is that the figure finally emerging from OMB is usually not far from what the division itself has asked for. Division personnel involved in budget making reported that their usual practice was to attempt to expand the organization's budget only by small increments. One recent AAG went so far as to remark of his own budgetary requests, "I think [what we get] is just about right. I don't really know what we'd *do* with many more men. Besides, they're not even *useful* until they've been trained a couple of years." In one very recent budget cycle the division broke with its common practice and requested a relatively large increment of funds. But this was a departure, according to a front office spokesman, due in large part to nonrecurrent circumstances: to a desire to recoup personnel losses that the division had been suffering through attrition and inflation and to the manpower requirements of an unusually large case.

The division justifies its requested increase in terms of new lawyers needed for general or special enforcement duties, more clerical personnel, salary raises, or, occasionally, office rental space and other expenses entailed in the opening of a new field office. Approximately 85 percent of the division's budget consists of personnel expenses, and one section chief gave the view from his office on how budgetary requests for new personnel usually came about. Once a year, he said, he and his fellow section chiefs re-

ceived a call from the front office, asking, "Hey, _____, you need
more lawyers this year?" The section chief further noted that his
"yes" or "no" answer to this question constituted his whole participation in the budgetary process, and that he almost always got
what he asked for. Budget officers confirmed this general description of the process; the bulk of the division's budget, they agreed,
originates in the organization's particular manpower requirements
at a particular time rather than in any comprehensive planning for
the division's future enforcement directions. The planning that
does occur is less likely to be a systematic review of resource requirements in all areas than it is to be a projection of costs for some
specific new enforcement activity, such as the establishment of a
new field office or a new prosecutorial unit.

The division's budget is subject to formal approval by the attorney general's office, and the department does attempt to exercise
some control over expenditure levels and resource allocation. But
as one division budget officer remembers his dealings with the
department, the cuts and reallocations made by the AAG's office
are usually small and do not stem from substantial questions about
the division's enforcement policies. "We've never been formally
cut," he recalled of his tenure,

. . . but there have been a couple of negotiations. There was one
dispute over a rearrangement of funds—how much was going to
go into various staff benefits and how much into transportation
expenses. And once, a couple of years ago, everyone was cut except the FBI. But that was Vietnam—it didn't have anything to do
with us. And that's about all.

In other words, when the division's requests are cut, the reason is
more likely to be overall budgetary stringency than a response to
any action that the division itself has taken; and when funds are
reallocated, it seems not to be in a way that calls into question the
division's decisions about where to put enforcement resources.

A Department of Justice budget officer confirmed that the department's oversight of division budgets by no means amounted to
the kind of programmatic control that a budget analyst might
desire:

The division's programs are uncontrollable. . . . Budgeting has
never been done on a programmatic basis. . . . The division has
always behaved the same way; they've gotten a little better, but

their justifications are so weak, and they ramble. . . . But they're cut less than the other divisions. AGs are very subjective about these things. . . . So we just try to *improve* their justifications.

So the department's own budget staff also sees the division's requests as particularistically arrived at and not easily subject to much tampering.

This same kind of slightly exasperated acceptance of the division's presentations marks the attitudes and actions of the Office of Management and Budget, which possesses significant formal power to change the amount and nature of the division's requests. A recent OMB examiner of the Justice Department's budget reported that OMB does not in fact exercise much of this power, and he explained his own reasons for this self-restraint:

Examination of the Antitrust Division budget is by and large cursory, though it varies with the head of the Antitrust Division. . . . But he's usually a man of outstanding academic stature. . . . And it's sort of "sacrosanct" in the Department of Justice.
But also, relative to the totals, eight or nine million dollars in the Antitrust Division isn't large, so we tend to spend the most effort where we can have the most impact.
It would be hard to reduce *or* increase the budget significantly. While the business community has on the whole accepted the need for this concern, I've sensed that there would be strong opposition to much of an increase. So the division *itself* doesn't ask for more. One reason is that it's highly specialized, and the attorneys and economists need to be sharp and gain experience before they face the antitrust bar. And lots of time is spent in data collection. So most assistant attorneys general say they couldn't *absorb* more than a 10 to 15 percent increase, and we agree; we'd turn down any more than that.
But none has *asked* for more; sometimes we try to get them to ask for more than they *do*. . . . One reason is that most of *us* believe that government antitrust enforcement efforts are inadequate, if anything. There's so much that tends to centralize this economy. . . . One of the constraints is that unless there's a major depression, and people start looking for a scapegoat, there's no one to push for it. . . .
The Antitrust Division makes things unusual. It's technical, it's small, and it has limited resources. We try to keep up, but we see it less than other parts of the Department of Justice. . . . We've never disapproved their budget or made them cut things out. They're even isolated within the department. I remember once going down there to discuss their judgments section. I managed to let them know about our concern: The court has often vested in the division responsibility for following through, and they haven't

used enough resources. They heard me, but I'm not sure they *did* anything. One year later they did beef it up, but I'm pretty sure *we* didn't have anything to do with it. . . .

Including the fall hearings, I meet with them only three times a year and make only five or ten phone calls, I'm ashamed to say. I always mean to get down there more. And not all those phone calls count. Sometimes another agency wants information and does it through us. I guess they *are* sort of unique. The Antitrust Division really leads a charmed life down there.

The examiner's explanation listed a complex set of reasons why he allowed the division the luxury of its "charmed life" among executive agencies and even within the Justice Department. First, the division is protected by its small size from the scrutiny of people who take the monetary size of the matters they are dealing with to be the major measure of their importance. The budget examiner saw this small size as in part the consequence of division self-restraint—a restraint that, as the examiner pointed out, is too marked to be explained solely as a reaction to constraints OMB itself is prepared to place on division requests. The examiner suspected that the restraint is due in part to a division perception that the general political climate would be hostile to large increases in division activity; the examiner knew that the restraint also stemmed from the organization's view of the nature and technical requirements of its task.

Second, the organization seems protected by a consensus in OMB that the division is doing a basically good thing, the more of which—under the present circumstances—the better. And it should be noted that on the one recent occasion when the division did ask for an unusually large increment of funds, OMB cut the request more heavily than usual but still was willing to allow the organization more than its standard "10 to 15 percent." Finally, the budget examiner was persuaded of the relatively high caliber of antitrust personnel and of the technical nature of the field, and these opinions of his gave him no great confidence in his general ability to prescribe for the division.

OMB has occasionally tried to impose more rigorous budgetary controls on the division. One of these attempts was the result of President Lyndon Johnson's desire to institute the now famous Planning-Programming-Budgeting System.[1] The purpose of the new system was to force the agencies to organize their expenditures in categories that corresponded to the agencies' major purposes and thus to be able to judge these expenditures in a more rigorous fashion. The budget examiner explained what the division's response had been to this reorganization:

We never did get them to see what we were talking about. See, here's their old line-item budget. And here's their new budget. Now they're dividing their expenses into a "conduct" category and a "structure" category. "Structure" is mainly their merger cases. But what's the relation between the two? How do they make their trade-offs? We had more trouble down there. . . . We never could get them to consider a whole range of alternative means for achieving their goals. After a couple of years, we just gave up on them.

Division personnel who participated in this budgetary interlude agree that OMB did not achieve what it set out to do. OMB simply could not understand, they say, that long-range planning and trade-offs of the desired type were impossible in the context of the division's complex goals, its system of information gathering, and the imperatives of prosecution.

In other words, when OMB tried to gain greater control over the division's allocation of resources through PPBS, it failed. Disappointments of this type certainly occurred in places other than the Antitrust Division when the PPBS experiment was made.[2] It is not that the division was unique in its resistance or in the difficulty of describing its mission in suitably precise terms; it is simply that the PPBS experiment in the division did not leave OMB personnel with any expanded notion of the possibilities for exercising much control over the division through its budget.

Very recently, another attempt at budget rationalization has affected the division—this time through the system called "management by objective," a system less ambitious than PPBS but similar in its desire to make the budgeting process more explicitly goal-directed. But viewing the prospects for the new system, a more recent budget examiner for the division in OMB echoed the words of his predecessor:

I'm concerned that their resource allocation now is just by cases. Now I'm just asking them for more analysis; the first step is to have them be more introspective. . . . They all feel that the laws are chiseled in stone, and they *know* how to enforce them. . . . But in the Antitrust Division, they're all lawyers; you can't tell them how to run their shop.

So the budgeting process in the executive branch has not come to serve as a significant independent determinant of division policy.

One budget examiner in OMB said that though OMB did not exercise much control over the division's budget, someone else did. "It's Congress that controls the Antitrust Division appropriation," he asserted, "not the Department of Justice or the Budget Office. It's the subcommittee." Yet to judge from reports of this congressional scrutiny and from the evidence of the hearings of the relevant House subcommittee, this control, too, is considerably less specific than one might expect.

This assessment is disputed by one ex–assistant attorney general. "Oh no," he said. "Rooney [John Rooney of New York, until recently the subcommittee chairman] is very tough."[3] On the other hand, the ex-AAG remarked, "[He] makes a lot of noise. But he *knows* we're not overbudgeted."

In recent years, the assistant attorney general of the division has each year made a similar appearance before the subcommittee.[4] The appearance, to judge by the written transcript, is not a long one, and the scripts of the appropriations hearings vary very little from year to year. The chairman may make a comment about an item of division behavior that has recently appeared in the press. There has often been attention called to the fact that the subcommittee has traditionally been kind to the division, rarely cutting its requests. (The division's budget has in fact declined once during the past fifteen years.)

The committee, led by the chairman, has usually asked the AAG four kinds of questions: (1) How many cases have been brought in the past year? (2) What proportion of those cases brought has been won? (3) What has been the severity of punishments meted out to individuals in criminal cases—has anyone gone to prison, and for how long? (4) What fines and damages have been collected during the year? These questions have occurred in almost all of the recent hearings.

Most of the time, some subcommittee member has expressed

dissatisfaction with the division's answers to one or more of these questions; he is upset that the number of cases brought has declined in comparison with the number of cases brought in some past year, or he is disappointed that fines collected in a given case did not even cover what the division estimates to have been the costs of prosecution. And such questions and comments constitute almost the whole of the policy direction imparted during the hearings. One recent appropriations hearing, on the appropriation for fiscal year 1975, differed markedly from its near predecessors because the division was asking for a much larger than usual appropriation increase. Almost certainly as a consequence, the subcommittee did recommend significant cuts. But even here, the policy directives that emerged from the hearing were no different or clearer.

Each hearing usually contains one or two questions about specific cases or policies. There have been questions about why the division has objected to a railroad merger that promises lower rates for farm shippers,[5] why the division has chosen to prosecute a farm association that seems exempt under the antitrust laws,[6] why the division favors a deregulation of stock commission rates that may raise prices for small investors,[7] why businessmen feel so harassed by the division.[8] These tend to be questions skeptical of division aggressiveness or of the primacy of the goal of promoting competition; when such questions occur, the AAG responding almost invariably states his disagreement with the premise of the questions and gives no sign that he will in the future take the congressman's concerns to heart. More rarely, there is a question suggesting that the division be more rather than less aggressive—there was a recent question, for instance, about why the division was not investigating what seemed to be a failure of one of its consent decrees to restore competitive conditions. When this kind of question occurs, the AAG gives indications that he will indeed be responsive to the congressman's concern.[9]

So there is expressed responsiveness only to those questions that ask that the division do more of what it is doing. More important, though, such questions are few. The policy categories that appear more regularly and frequently in the hearings are those of cases brought, proportion of cases won, severity of sentences, and amount of fines and damages.

One might think that the division would certainly take action during the course of the year to provide answers to those questions that are almost invariably asked about its performance, but in fact it is difficult to find any conscious, specific organizational response of this kind. That is by no means to assert that Congress exercises no influence at all through the hearings process. The desires of Congress as expressed by the subcommittee—desires that can perhaps be summarized as a wish for "more and better cases" —must be assumed to be a powerful constraint on any division executive who might otherwise try to replace that loose standard with another set of goals. So the subcommittee most probably provides an external reinforcement for the staff lawyers' general notions of what antitrust enforcement should be like. But the effect of this potential constraint is very hard to judge, since we have seen that there has rarely been a recent assistant attorney general who seems to have wanted to make such major changes. And conversely, when Assistant Attorney General Turner wanted to change the division's methods, he was not deterred by fears of the subcommittee.

There is a more important reason why one cannot easily say that the subcommittee exercises much of a direct policy influence on the division: The questions the subcommittee almost invariably asks, and the criteria those questions imply to be the proper ones for measuring the division's performance, are not very different from and no more precisely ordered than those used by the lawyers themselves in making their individual decisions. The subcommittee's publicly stated criteria—the standards of "more and better cases"—are not only roughly the same as the division's own, they are also potentially contradictory in the same way the division's are. An organization operating solely by the rule of "Bring more cases" would choose its cases very differently from one working exclusively by the rule of "Win a very high proportion of those cases you *do* bring." Similarly, the rules of "Send as many people as you can to prison" and "Collect more in fines and damages from each case than it costs you to prosecute the cases" provide other distinctive, potentially contradictory guides to prosecution decisions.

In fact, these potential contradictions pose no great operational problem for the division. Most cases are brought without thought of these potential choices, and in cases where such a choice does have to be made—as in a decision about whether to bring a case that might well be lost—it is made very much in light of the particular facts and problems involved rather than according to any general policy. For the subcommittee to change this policy of particularism would require at the very least a clear expression of which standards were to be given precedence in planning prosecution strategy. And, as is shown by the unordered presence of all these criteria together in questions asked at almost every individual hearing, no such clarity exists.

Aside from this lack of a clear preference, there is a further reason why it is hard to point to a distinct collective influence that the subcommittee has on the division's performance. As the subcommittee itself has pointed out repeatedly, that body only rarely recommends cutting the division's appropriation. When attempts to cut the appropriation request have in fact occurred, they have been prompted in large part by concerns—such as inflation—that are external to the performance of the division itself. Further, the subcommittee members have usually felt bound to appear in these hearings as public partisans of the general goals of the division and of "the fine job the division does." These circumstances do not provide any special incentive to the division to make major policy changes in light of recurring subcommittee pressures, even if these pressures were clear enough to give one a definite idea of what the desired changes were.

In fact, fear of the subcommittee does not seem to play much of a role at all in determining the division's actual day-to-day operating decisions. The front office reports that it does worry, as each budget season nears, about how good the "cases brought" and "won-lost" figures will look to the subcommittee. But even if one granted that this fear were well grounded, one would have to note that the front office seems not to have much success or even to exert much effort at altering the staff lawyers' conduct in response to this executive concern. As one section chief explained,

These case figures don't mean a thing to me. We don't rely much on these figures. For instance, one year in the _____ section we filed twenty cases. But fourteen of them followed from one investigation, in the _____ industry. That was only *one* case, really. I know, each year someone in the front office will start telling us, "The end of the fiscal year is coming, and if we don't have fifty-five cases filed, we're in trouble." And the reaction of everyone from section chief on down to that kind of stuff is to *laugh*. *I* don't care what the statistics are.

In short, it is hard to see differences that the congressional appropriations process actually makes in the division's performance because one cannot observe the subcommittee articulating operating principles different from the division's own, imposing sanctions for disobedience to congressional principles, or creating any great fear of or allegiance to those principles among the division's operatives. The subcommittee reinforces the lawyers' predilections rather than voicing a clear alternative to them.

So the division seems to have achieved a measure of safety in its budgetary dealings: It is protected from selective budgetary attacks by its small size, the technical nature of its task, and its broadly popular goal. But there remains the question of why the division's budget, in spite of its most recent growth, has not increased even more rapidly. Part of the reason seems to lie in the fact that each party to its budget-making process anticipates, perhaps incorrectly, the actions and attitudes of others. Some division members think that under normal circumstances, a larger budget request would be unacceptable to OMB. OMB says that though *it* might favor more money for the division, it fears that too large a request would be unacceptable to "general business opinion," which would make itself felt through Congress. In fact none of these external parties whose opinions are so much anticipated has taken overt, successful action against division requests for increases.

Another part of the answer, therefore, must lie—and does lie —in the division's conception of its task. The division does operate largely on a case-by-case basis rather than through comprehensive planning of its enforcement strategy. On occasion, the presence of an unusually demanding case or project or some external or procedural factor—staff losses as a result of inflation or changes in penalties that promise to induce more defendants actually to opt for full-length trials—may lead the division to request a larger-than-usual increase in funds. But in the absence of such special factors, the organization has not shown itself to be in the habit of envisioning broadly expanding fiscal needs. The relative stability of the division's budget stems as much from its own methods of operation as from the pressures of a hostile environment. And the example of the division's recent success at resisting its own appropriations subcommittee and obtaining a relatively large increase also suggests the importance of internal expectations rather than external pressures in determining the organization's resources.[10]

The second point about control over the division through its budget is simpler and perhaps even more important. The agencies that supervise the division's budget do not use their budgetary control in behalf of any systematic antitrust enforcement strategies of their own. Those that have, on occasion, tried at least to affect the division's goal-formation process by demanding increased clarity have by and large failed in the attempt. The power of the purse, in this instance, is far from the ability to direct policy.

Legislative Oversight

If neither the executive branch nor Congress chooses to exercise substantial policy control over the division through its budget, one might nevertheless expect them to try to direct in other ways, for example, through the oversight process. One might suppose Congress to be particularly active in this regard. This is not by any means to say that presidents have never interested themselves in the subject of antitrust enforcement; as will be discussed later in this chapter, presidents have indeed found occasion to try to influence particular cases. Further, assistant attorneys general have sometimes obtained the explicit approval of a president's close advisers before embarking on a particular kind of antitrust campaign. Nevertheless, it is fair to say that presidents in postwar America have not made antitrust enforcement an object of their sustained or systematic intervention.

By contrast, the House and Senate subcommittees under whose jurisdiction the division falls do give systematic attention to antitrust. The Senate Subcommittee on Antitrust and Monopoly of the Committee on the Judiciary, to take the stronger case, has gained a reputation for sustained activity. It regularly holds major hearings on problems of competition in the economy as a whole and in various industries, and in these hearings at least some attention has usually been paid to the Antitrust Division's operations in the area under consideration. Moreover, even apart from the specific investigations of which these hearings are a part, the staff members of the subcommittee report close relations and frequent contacts between themselves and the division.

When the subcommittee holds hearings on competitive conditions in some area of the economy or on a proposed piece of antitrust-relevant legislation, the division's assistant attorney general usually makes an appearance, and almost all the questions put to the AAGs fall into one of three categories. First, an AAG may be asked his opinion of a proposed legislative change—a change proposed by the division itself or one originating in the subcommittee. If the division has not suggested the change it is quite possible that there may be a public disagreement about the need for it. In one such hearing in 1961, Assistant Attorney General Lee Loevinger disagreed with the proposal under consideration for a special antitrust act to govern the drug industry;[11] in another hearing, a similar skepticism was expressed about the need for specific laws covering television network advertising.[12] In these cases, an AAG or other division spokesman gives his dissenting opinion without encountering sustained hostile questioning.

Second, an AAG may be asked for a legal opinion—usually about whether an alleged anticompetitive condition is within the reach of existing interpretations of antitrust law. During a set of 1965 Senate hearings on economic concentration, for instance, Assistant Attorney General William Orrick was questioned about the status of potential competition arguments under the Clayton Act and, more generally, about the adequacy of the laws in the face of conglomerate mergers. Orrick replied with summaries of the division's opinion and a caution that the question of the applicability of various theories in these cases could be answered adequately only in light of the particular facts of each situation. Occasionally a new legal approach is suggested to the division: In the same portion of these economic concentration hearings, for instance, the subcommittee's chief economist asked whether the Sherman Act could be newly applied to conglomerate mergers. Orrick replied that the possibility should be investigated. But in general, these exchanges on matters of legal theory have had the character of presentation of data rather than of pressure by the subcommittee to change an opinion expressed by an AAG.

Third, the subcommittee does often ask in detail about division policy toward some case or industry or set of industries. Sometimes the division appears simply resistant to such questions. When asked why his predecessors had not begun sooner to prosecute conglomerate cases, Assistant Attorney General Orrick replied, "It's always helpful to have that foresight."[13] When asked in 1968 by senators of conflicting views what the division would do in the field of television network advertising, then–acting Assistant Attorney General Edwin Zimmerman repeated, "As I have attempted to say twice in my prepared statement, we have no view one way or the other on whether we have an octopus or a pussycat here. We have to examine the facts and we have formed no judgment."[14] When chided on another occasion in 1965 for insufficient division activity in the field of foreign commerce, Zimmerman, then assistant to the AAG, simply did not concede that the problem of division behavior was as large as had been implied.[15] In another hearing in 1955, when Assistant Attorney General Stanley Barnes was accused of not following announced division policy concerning prefiling negotiations in a given case, he answered that he had his own criteria for deciding when these negotiations would be conducted and that the case in question simply had not met them.[16]

The division is not unvaryingly resistant to such questions. On the contrary, when the subcommittee has presented the division with information that the congressmen think worthy of investigation, the information is often received with a public expression of gratitude and a pledge to proceed with the work now at hand. And though the division resists public judgment on specific cases, it almost always answers that they are being looked into or should be looked into. So the division in these hearings often seems willing to be publicly prodded into further action, but the prodding that is accepted is of a general and sporadic sort in behalf of the goal of more prosecution.

Perhaps it is not surprising that the division is treated easily and with some delicacy in these public hearings. During their course, assistant attorneys general have repeatedly excused themselves from discussing particular case decisions in any detail.[17] They argue that these are prosecutorial matters to be held in confidence. In public senators accept this argument, and this public acceptance suggests that it might be naïve to judge the extent of the Senate's attempts to influence the division on the basis of public hearings alone. If senators do not want to be seen delving into the internal operations of a law enforcement agency, one should look to the more private contacts between the subcommittee and the division, not only by the senators but by the subcommittee's staff. And one should look not only to the relatively infrequent public hearings but to the day-to-day relations between staff and division.

The subcommittee staff does maintain extensive contacts of several kinds with the division, as one staff member pointed out:

We propose areas we want to look into, or [the subcommittee chairman] might express *his* wish in a certain area. . . . My job is sort of to "peer around the corner" and look for long-range projects. For instance, I'm planning fuel oil hearings. Or we might get mail suggesting areas—for instance, from shareholders of a small trucking company that's about to be bought up. Some of these things we send to the enforcement agencies. . . .

We can also produce publicity. . . . On hearings, if we *or* they think they ought to testify, we have contact. Sometimes we discuss on a philosophical level what's the right course for them to take. Sometimes they *don't* want to testify. Then we have to send a formal request, and it's very hard for them to say no.

But here's another kind of situation. They *wanted* to testify on the _____ bill, but of course they have to clear it through OMB and we knew the _____ Department was going to take an opposite position. Our job was to get OMB to allow *both* to testify and *not* designate either position as the "official" administration position beforehand. I did this partly through timing, partly through giving the AAG a "club" to use in discussions. So mostly our relations are informal and friendly.

We . . . talk to the regular lawyers, too. For instance, on the _____ amendment hearings. Or we write a general letter on a subject, including and evaluating the complaints we've received. Then the Antitrust Division guys meet with us. . . . On the _____ issue, we got compulsory licensing into the consent decree, and they were happy to do it.

This catalog of the varieties of communication with and influence upon the division is impressive. It includes not only suggesting areas where cases might lie and influencing the division's relations with other parts of the federal government but discussing the outcome of specific sets of cases as well. On the other hand, while one cannot take such statements as a full description of actual behavior, the subcommittee staff also makes clear that it feels definite constraints on its attempts to direct the division or to bring matters to the division's attention. One subcommittee staffer described and gave reasons for these restraints:

We don't do anything like keeping tabs on which cases we refer to them get taken up. All we ask for is reasoned evaluation, and we get it. . . .
     The Antitrust Division is unique. . . . Congress doesn't scrutinize it so much . . . because the appropriations are so small. . . . Also, this is . . . like the criminal law area. Congress has traditionally stayed out of prosecutorial things. . . . I would like to see more attention to the division's internal workings, because it's adjudicative in itself. But it's touchy, because it has criminal enforcement responsibilities, to have a political body oversee it. . . . For instance, [Senator Philip] Hart has done oversight in his other committees, but not this one. . . .
     Other members who are less supportive of the antitrust laws haven't exercised oversight either because (a) they don't control the staff, (b) they don't have enough time, and (c) they know that the Antitrust Division doesn't have many resources now. . . . Also, [Ralph] Nader is right: It is like "mother and apple pie. . . . "
     Also, the division has always been a blue chip organization ethically, and it's the same with the subcommittee staff. . . . Even before Hart, with [Senator Estes] Kefauver, the staff wasn't so "genteel," but it was known as independent, almost puritan. . . . From the outside, it seems as if the staffers are very political. Actually, what I've been impressed with is their high professional level. . . .
     It's an esoteric subject; it's really a guild operation. . . . And there haven't been any ideological clashes so far. . . . Intellectually, we're the same; we appreciate each other's problems. It's not like the other agencies we deal with, where (a) we don't know them so well, and (b) we oppose their views.

So the subcommittee's staff is indeed the main agent of this congressional oversight of the division, and staff contacts with the division are close, especially in the area of the division's relations with the rest of the government. But the staff feels that its oversight of the division is more limited than the oversight the subcommittee gives the other executive agencies under its jurisdiction. The staff has its own reasons for abstaining from closer scrutiny of the division's internal operations and says that the subcommittee's congressmen have yet other reasons for abstaining. For those sub-committee congressmen who consider themselves antitrust champions the goal is mainly to prod the division into more action, but such congressmen are constrained in their prodding not only by a fear of entanglement in prosecutorial matters but by a fundamental agreement with both the goals the division pursues and the general manner in which it pursues them. Those congressmen who are said to have less sympathy with aggressive antitrust enforcement seem nevertheless not to take persecution of the division as a major interest of theirs, because of the division's already small budget and because of the popularity of the general goal of antitrust enforcement. It has been claimed that the presence of these "opposing" members has in recent years prevented any further extensions of the antitrust laws themselves; in light of recent changes in consent decree and investigation procedures and antitrust penalties, this charge seems at best only partially justified.[18] But in any event, this hostility does not extend overtly to the internal operations of the division under existing laws.

The reasons the staff, as opposed to congressmen themselves, does not engage itself in any detailed or sustained administrative oversight are slightly more complicated. It is not simply that the staff fears to involve itself in prosecutorial matters. Indeed, the staff member quoted above asserted that the division should be thought of more as an administrative agency, subject to "normal" oversight, than it is now.

Instead, the staff treats the division's internal operations with some respect for other reasons. First, like the senators, they see the general goal of antitrust enforcement as widely popular. Further, they have in recent years been hired by senators with strong pro-antitrust views. Thus it is not surprising that they do not simply accept the existence of antitrust enforcement as a matter of political expediency but welcome it and try to encourage it.

But this explanation is not sufficient. Especially if the staff generally consists of antitrust advocates, one might expect them to want to intervene as much and as constructively as possible in the decisions that the division makes. The reason they say they do not do so more often seems to lie in their attitude toward what the staff member called the "professionalism" of the division.

The term "professionalism" is used as a word of praise by the subcommittee staff, and this is not surprising since the staff considers itself to be a "professional" rather than a "political" one. Its nonclerical personnel hold advanced degrees in law or economics. They call the division "professional," "blue chip," and "independent"; antitrust enforcement is labeled "esoteric" and a "guild" operation. These words are signs of another part of the staff's attitude toward the division: the notion that staff and division share not only an attachment to the same fundamental goals but a common notion, dictated by profession, of what constitutes proper procedure in pursuit of these goals. Because of its perception of the division's "professionalism," in other words, the staff thinks that the division will in general make decisions like those the staff itself would make if confronted with the same particular set of facts. This staff explanation does seem to conform to its behavior.

The subcommittee staff acts privately and through major public investigations to call possible cases to the division's attention. And the division, for reasons that were discussed in chapter 4, is not at all averse to receiving such information. But the subcommittee staff seems by and large satisfied that the "reasoned evaluation" the division gives this information is made in light of criteria that the subcommittee staff shares and approves of. This staff is, then, a group that has the incentives and the knowledge to oversee the division's operations in the most detailed and systematic manner; but for this group ideological and professional consensus makes the task of oversight one of reinforcing staff predilections rather than imposing any new ones.

Individual Interventions

Formal congressional oversight is not the only possible method of intervening in the division's case selection. The consensus on the general desirability of antitrust enforcement, it may be argued, makes frontal attacks costly, and the division's prosecutorial responsibilities limit the extent of overt public inquiry into its internal affairs. We might instead expect to find a pattern of private attempts to influence the outcome of individual cases—attempts that should be fairly frequent in light of the political resources and connections of the businessmen and their lawyers whose interests are affected by division actions.

For obvious reasons, information about such attempts to intervene is fragmentary and hard to interpret. First, people try to hide evidence of their own wrongdoing. Then there is the opposite bias: Much of the evidence on the topic of intervention in division cases comes from division staff lawyers whose recommendations to prosecute have been rejected by higher levels of the organization. Fortunately, we have a useful compilation of alleged improprieties in the Nader study group's *The Closed Enterprise System*, and the instances mentioned in this report can, with some later additions, form the basis of at least the beginnings of an analysis.[19]

The Closed Enterprise System lists thirty-two examples of improper influence on the division over the past twenty-five years, fourteen from Congress and eighteen from the executive branch —by the White House directly or through the attorney general. The head of the study group that prepared the report said in an interview that no such story that he had believed true was omitted from the report.

One interesting feature of these incidents is that even if every one of them represented a change made in the division's case selection process for reasons of personal or partisan interest, the number would still seem rather low for an agency without any particularly attentive popular interest in its specific decisions, and rather low for an agency dealing with rich companies, many of whom have or are thought to have well-established political connections with Congress or the executive branch. This preliminary verdict would be different if such incidents seemed to occur routinely in the "biggest" cases, either those involving the largest companies or those involving the most serious violations or possible penalties. But no such pattern appears. Sometimes the case in question is indeed a "big" one, but at other times influence seems to have been exerted simply because a congressman decided to involve himself in the fate of a constituent company of his, whether or not it was a large one in comparison to other companies investigated by the division.

An even more interesting feature of these reported attempts to influence the division is that they are often clearly unsuccessful. The following incident involved a congressman who might be presumed to have exceptional influence with the division:[20]

In the *Burlington Watch* case of the mid-fifties, [Representative Emmanuel] Celler's New York law firm represented Benrus, a competitor of the defendant. Benrus was unhappy with the practice of importers bringing in low jeweled (low duty) watches and "upjeweling" them here. They wanted this practice included in the complaint. . . . The Division received a letter from Celler, wearing his Congressional "hat," inquiring why this new count was not being included. A Division lawyer drafted a scathing reply, which Antitrust Chief Stanley Barnes chose not to send. No reply at all was sent to Celler and no follow-up was received from him.

There was no question, in this case, about whether the division was going to change its decision in response to the congressman's wishes; the only question was whether to chastise him or ignore him altogether.

Neither are all the reported incidents of attempted influence through the executive branch examples of success:[21]

On another case, the Schlitz Beer Company tried to quash the suit against its mergers with John Labatt, Ltd., and the Burgermeister Brewing Co., by sending a former General and former JFK campaign director to lobby. . . . When it failed, they obtained a second audience, *sans* General, but again without success. Yet the firm had been so confident of the outcome of these meetings that they suddenly found themselves unprepared for trial when it was scheduled a year and a half after the complaint had been filed. They sought a court extension—and failed once more.

Schlitz may have been placing its trust in an established structure of influence that accidentally and unaccountably failed in this one instance, or it may have been acting on very bad advice; what seems clear is that the company did not succeed in changing the division's decision.

In addition to this category of clear failure, there is a category of attempts that may have been successful (the outcome was what the petitioner wanted, though it is not always clear whether his intervention was crucial in forming the decision) but where even if the division was somehow influenced by an external party, the decision not to file a case seems to have been based not on "political clout" in any narrow sense but at least in part on an argument a petitioner presented about the importance of some goal he thought should enter into antitrust enforcement strategy. For instance:[22]

Senators [Abraham] Ribicoff (D.-Conn.) and [John] McClellan (D.-Ark.) urged that Justice not file suit, as the Antitrust Division intended, against General Electric's take-over of a household appliance company. . . . They claimed that plants employing 1000 in New Britain, Connecticut, and 600 in Fort Smith, Arkansas, would shut down if there were no merger. No case was filed.

There are several other incidents of this kind reported, a number of them during the tenure from 1965 to 1966 of Attorney General Nicholas deB. Katzenbach. As the Nader study group puts it, "'Antipoverty' arguments had great appeal to Katzenbach. . . . "[23] In other words, there are a good number of cases in which even if the attempt at influence was successful, the failure to prosecute stemmed not simply from conventional corruption but from real differences in substantive positions about the proper role of antitrust in promoting a variety of economic goals.

But in fact, it is hard to know whether such attempts have been successful. When an outsider tries to intervene in a division prosecution, it is not always clear that the decision not to prosecute comes because of that outside intervention. Some ex-members of the division have said, for instance, that some cases in which political pressure has been alleged were instead turned down because an assistant attorney general has simply presented an inferior case at conferences with defense counsel in the attorney general's offices, and the attorney general has had good reason to believe the defense facts and arguments superior. In addition, reinterviews with lawyers involved in some of these cases reveal that the case outcomes were influenced not simply by outside politics but also by doubts in the minds of at least some division members themselves. Thus one lawyer commented on a case in which the division

was accused of improper leniency: "I don't know where he [refer-
ring to the Nader report] got that. That wasn't just politics. Sure,
they tried to persuade us, but you have to remember that we
weren't sure then. At that time it was a serious legal question
whether that practice was to be permitted; we didn't know whether we could *win* that case."

In other words, there is some indication that outside influence
of this type is exercised most successfully when at least some inside the division have their own doubts as to the illegality of the
offenses alleged and the chances of winning in court. As one ex–
assistant attorney general put it, "Where the attorney general has
been interested in a particular case, it's never been a question of a
clear violation, never something about which I had no doubt."

So the incidence of improper outside influence in these matters
is rather low when one considers the questions of actual success
and of the division's own certainty about its legal position. And
judgment is not made simpler by the recent allegations concerning
1971 White House interventions in the division's cases against the
International Telephone and Telegraph Company. From the records made public so far, there is no doubt that the White House
tried to influence the division not to appeal decisions against the
government in the ITT cases. It seems equally clear that there was
disagreement within the division over its chances of ultimate success, that the White House interest was based not mainly on considerations of personal or partisan favor but on more general views
about the proper status of "bigness" as an object of antitrust attack, and that the most overt attempt by President Richard Nixon
personally to order then-Attorney General Richard Kleindienst not
to appeal these cases was a failure. This is not to say that the views
held by the White House did not finally make themselves felt. It is
only to say that in this incident as in other reported incidents, the
motives involved cannot be clearly judged to have been those of
classic corruption and that the division had its own reasons for
uncertainty as to its proper course of action.[24]

There seems little doubt that sometimes a case is "fixed," sometimes through Congress or an AAG and his staff and sometimes
through the White House and the attorney general, and it seems
reasonable to believe that high officials in the division sometimes

give excessive weight to outsiders' arguments. But as far as one can judge, these types of behavior seem to occur more often where the law itself and thus the obligation to prosecute are in significant doubt. And perhaps even more important, one cannot say that these incidents occur very often at all. Since this is the case, it seems not too perverse to argue that the question to be asked is not why this kind of political influence is exercised over the division or what forms it takes; instead, the question might be why no more of such influence seems to exist.

First of all, it must be noted that reports of corruption or improper influence in the division rarely involve improprieties by individual staff lawyers—though a few lawyers have reported attempts by the defense to influence them improperly. This pattern might, of course, reflect a bias in the sources from which information of this type usually comes. Still, the opinion is almost universal among alumni, defense counsel in general, and outside observers of the division as well that the division staff lawyers are notably honest.

Part of this behavior could be explained by the dearth of opportunities for the corruption of staff lawyers. Few of them work closely enough and often enough with one firm or one set of defense counsel to develop the kind of personal relationships conducive to the asking and giving of favors. Furthermore, the lawyers do not usually work alone, especially on large matters. Unless they are already in trial, they do not usually spend protracted periods of time away from the supervision of their colleagues and superiors. Finally, the staff lawyers must repeatedly give those colleagues and superiors fairly elaborate justifications for their opinions and recommendations.

But such explanations are not wholly satisfactory. First, there are the cases, especially small investigations, where a lawyer does work largely alone. Second, the division does contain industry specialists who deal with one firm frequently or for extended periods of time; yet there is simply no evidence that increased frequency of contact results in a significant and unusual amount of corruption. And finally, the law's ambiguity in many cases would seem to permit giving plausible justification for opinions that have in fact been bought. So an additional explanation must be adduced.

An explanation is also needed for assistant attorneys general. Unlike the staff lawyers, AAGs and attorneys general have indeed been accused of corruption or at least of systematically, improperly undervaluing the worth of antitrust prosecution. And certainly one can see why it would be both easier and more attractive to a higher official to tamper improperly with a case. An AAG or an attorney general can, in theory, make his decisions alone and give relatively cursory reasons for them. Because these high-level decisions and reasons are less subject to review and collective scrutiny, and because high-level officials are more visible to outsiders, someone who wants to influence the outcome of a case might well prefer to approach a high official rather than a staff lawyer. And such an approach is made easier by a standing policy in the department regarding antitrust cases: Before the final decision is made to file a noncriminal case, defense counsel and outsiders are allowed, if they wish, to present their views to the AAG. Finally, these higher officials are political appointees, and this fact might be thought to open to them an increased receptivity to political argument and a larger and better variety of potential rewards.

One can speculate on the reasons why even with these higher officials the successful approaches do not occur more often. One reason seems to be that a reputation for receptivity to these approaches holds not only opportunities but serious political dangers; public allegations of impropriety of this type are extremely damaging. Another reason for the restraint seems to be that in fact not many antitrust defendants have enough political resources for department officials to warrant the risks involved in this type of dealing. Antitrust defendants may have significant political connections; but even when they do, they also have suppliers, customers, and competitors who may be only too glad to see the case at hand go forward. These other interested parties may not be without potential countervailing resources of their own.

But as with the staff, these factors do not fully explain the relative rarity of such interventions. Another factor seems to play a part in the division stance toward outside influence: the close connections that not only staff lawyers but assistant attorneys general and their staffs maintain with their colleagues in the private antitrust bar. It may be argued that these professional associations, both direct and indirect, can themselves be a significant source of influence peddling and corruption. But they also provide a publicity that to a large extent compensates for a lack of detailed attention by the general public and that staff lawyers and division executives alike regard as a powerful constraint on their actions.

The division maintains what must be described as very close relations with the antitrust bar, both institutionally and through the personal relationships of its individual lawyers. First of all, division lawyers leave to become private antitrust lawyers themselves; AAGs and their staff also leave to go or return to private practice. These alumni keep up with ex-colleagues within the division. Furthermore, division lawyers come into frequent contact with various members of the private antitrust bar who represent firms the division investigates. In addition, lawyers who have entered the division after some private practice—often the AAG or parts of his personal staff—are acquanted with the antitrust lawyers they met when they practiced privately.

These professional relationships are sustained ones in part because the antitrust bar remains relatively small; the Antitrust Section of the American Bar Association listed for 1976 the names of 10,568 regular members, up dramatically from only 6,500 as late as 1971.[25] The section holds regular meetings, as do the local Bar Association sections in large cities. The meetings are attended by private and government antitrust lawyers, and the contacts maintained through the association are not only professional but institutional. Recent division executives have made a considerable effort to cultivate and extend professional communication between the division and the private bar. "After all," as one staff member explained this effort, "they're our best enforcers." Most recent Bar Association section meetings have been marked by a speech from the incumbent AAG or one of his top staff, and the AAG's speeches are often reprinted in one of the antitrust bar's periodicals. Not only these speeches and the journals themselves but the government decisions and actions reported by the Commerce Clearing House and the Bureau of National Affairs are read with regularity by private bar and division personnel alike. They are considered by division members to be an important way for the private bar to keep watch over the division's actions. "They know what we're doing and we know what they're doing," as one division lawyer put it. "We all read the same opinions and the same journals."

Besides this common reading, listening, and meeting, the division and the private bar also constitute two parts of a single job market. The reputations of the division's younger attorneys become known to the private bar either through personal contact in the course of various dealings or through older supervising attorneys who have remained in the division. And though there seems to be some disagreement among the private bar on just how high is the caliber of the young lawyers the division produces, division lawyers and private ones seem to agree about the criteria for judging professional competence. During the time in which this project's first interviews were conducted, a number of young division lawyers left for private practice; they were among the first of their entering classes to be hired away, and they were all people who had been acknowledged by their division colleagues to be good antitrust lawyers in the organization's sense of the term. As one private lawyer, a division alumnus, put it when asked about congruence of standards, "If I were looking for an antitrust lawyer now, *sure* I'd ask the opinions of the section chiefs I respected when I was there."

No one in the division reported that staff lawyers had been induced to recommend against prosecution because of friendships developed through these various professional channels. What was often reported was the opposite situation. Staff lawyers and private attorneys, it was often said, establish mutually profitable relationships in which the staff lawyer receives information about possible violations committed by competitors, suppliers, or customers of the firm a private lawyer represents; the private lawyer acts in hopes of increasing his chances that the division will prosecute the offending party.

Such contacts occur at the level of the AAG's office, as well. One private lawyer, not an alumnus, who enjoyed rather close relations with the top staff of one particular administration, explained how he was about to try to influence them:

The division isn't at all corrupt. One tries to persuade them and show determination—not ask for favors. . . .

I'm handling a client now who wants to sue the wholly owned European subsidiary of an American company for violating the American laws. I *will* go to Washington and try to persuade _____ that the *government* should take the case. . . . I know _____, _____, and _____ in the division. I know _____ from having a case against him, and _____ was with a firm in this city, and a friend, and _____ is a personal friend. . . . One *can* do that kind of lobbying.

I was thinking about it—what arguments to use with _____— while I was shaving this morning. I'll probably say that since the Common Market is going to be the thing of the future, and there are many complaints about our exporting American capital and American jobs, this is the time to get some control of it. . . .

That's what good lobbying is—not asking for favors, but getting inside the other guy's head, figuring out what would be good for *him*. . . .

Obviously, one must assume that this norm of persuasion rather than asking for favors is sometimes violated. Furthermore, as it will later be argued, the division's close connections with its private adversaries may impose important costs of its own on antitrust enforcement. But if one is interested in the extent to which political corruption stops prosecutions, one must say that professional norms do exert substantial control and that they provide yet another set of constraints that reduce the level of more obvious kinds of corruption.

8
Organization and Public Policy

The Antitrust Division is organized for prosecuting. It relies on courts as the arbiters of its decisions, and it has taken this reliance to require that most of the agency's work should be done by lawyers. These lawyers do not see themselves as holding significant administrative discretion; their view of their relationship to the courts prevents that. But this limitation is taken to confer a corresponding freedom—a freedom from the obligation to take a comprehensive view of the merits of possible antitrust cases. For division staff, in other words, restricted administrative discretion brings with it a corresponding freedom to advocate.

This view of the organization's task is encouraged by the system of inducements and constraints the division offers to its individual members. As we have seen, the nature of the information available to the staff and the career satisfactions open to them make prosecution both a difficult and a highly valued activity. This ethos has important effects on the division's relations with its potential client groups, its professional reference group, and other governmental bodies, and it also plays an important part in determining what ideas about competition and the nation's economic health the division promotes.

First of all, on the matter of relations with outsiders, the division staff's stance as a group of lawyers and prosecutors has important effects on its general attitude toward the businessmen with whom it comes into contact. The division staff has a reputation for being relatively "clean," for being hard to influence through pressures from the private interests it deals with, and for not treating them with systematic leniency. One explanation that the staff itself offers for this sanitary atmosphere is a type of opportunity theory: The division, so the argument goes, deals with no one firm or industry frequently enough for systematic corruption or clientalist sympathies to emerge. Furthermore, the close presence of colleagues and the necessity to make detailed justifications for one's opinions reduce the opportunities for clientalism and corruption of a more ad hoc variety.

This explanation, as we have seen, is helpful but not sufficient. It is true that most division personnel have limited contact with any one potential client group, that they do not tend to see themselves as allocating scarce resources among competing private interests, and that the organization's decisions are indeed made after much discussion and justification. On the other hand, there is enough division of labor and enough isolation, especially in some relatively specialized areas, to permit more staff corruption than seems to exist. The organization of much of the division by commodity jurisdiction, for instance, and the length of individual cases, would seem to provide opportunity for closer ties and more sympathetic behavior than an observer can discover.

Therefore one needs an additional explanation for the distance that seems to prevail between the staff and the private parties it deals with, and this additional explanation seems to lie in the lawyers' view that they are adversarial prosecutors. This model of proper behavior entails contempt for organization members who succumb to improper pressures or inducements or even for those who too easily abandon their partisan roles out of a simple appreciation for their adversaries' point of view. And the prevalence of such an ethos means that the formal structure of the opportunities for corruption or co-optation simply will not produce their full quota of tainted behavior. As we have seen, considerations certainly do exist that will dissuade the staff from recommending prosecution of what it thinks may be a winnable case, but these considerations almost never include a simple regard for the well-being of the firm or industry in question, at least not in the same terms in which a defendant himself would understand that well-being. And if the self-image of the prosecutor acts less powerfully on higher-level members of the organization, it is still powerful enough—not only to the organization's executives but to an attentive staff, Congress, and private bar—so that the violation is likely to be discovered, and the costs of violation are likely to be high.

The division's status as a legal, prosecutorial organization also affects the type of control that other governmental bodies exercise over it. It is widely admitted that direct control over division policy by Congress or the executive branch may occur but is a relatively infrequent thing. As with division-business relationships, observers offer various explanations for the phenomenon. For one thing, the organization is small, and this small size is said to make the division "harmless" or at least insignificant in the eyes of potential controllers, except where a particularly large and visible individual case is involved. For another, the division acts in behalf of a goal others in government think is widely popular. As we have seen, this perceived consensus not only protects the division from much overt public attack but significantly raises the potential costs of more private interference.

Once again, though, such explanations are not quite sufficient. The division may escape routine attention because its budget is small, but the budget has remained small in good part because the constraints of prosecution usually limit the size of the requests the organization makes. On the one recent occasion when the division asked for an unusually large increase in its budget, the barriers to the increase proved fragile. Furthermore, it is not simply that "enemies" of antitrust enforcement feel constrained in their attacks by the general popularity of antitrust goals; as we have seen, friends of this generally popular position also feel limited in the extent to which they can properly intervene in or oversee the division's actual operations. Once again a supplementary explanation is needed, and once again it appears that the explanation lies in the agency's status as a prosecutorial organization. This status, and not simply the popularity of antitrust aims, creates either a genuine belief in the division's independence or a certain caution about compromising that independence. This status also limits the demands the division makes on other parts of the government and the frequency with which its actions make it an object of real controversy.

In its relations with business and with the rest of government, then, the division gains considerable independence because of its prosecutorial status and its participation in the legal system of which prosecutors are a part. In these cases, aggressive prosecution and acknowledged professionalism contribute to the same effect.

But the third public with which the division deals is the antitrust bar as a whole; and in its dealing with this public the imperatives of prosecution and those of professionalism provide guides that sometimes conflict. It may be argued that the division's consciousness of an attentive private bar has some "conservatizing" effects on the organization, whether through division lawyers' conscious decisions or not. First of all, a professional self-image limits the kinds of information that the division will gather and consider useful for purposes of prosecution. One can imagine a division that required less information than the present one does as a basis for investigation, a division that devoted more of its resources to planning and creating its own opportunities for prosecution. Without making a judgment at this point on the relative merits and defects of this alternative strategy, one can certainly say that the division does not follow it; the division concentrates massively on information that already bears a fairly direct relation to some specific antitrust violation. This strategy seems to stem in at least two ways from the prevalent notion of what is required of a professional in this field. First, it is felt that being a prosecutor implies limits: Organization members stated that they were prosecutors rather than policemen and that they preferred to "take their cases as given." Second, they professed a contempt—and a consciousness of their profession's contempt—for the practice of using the laws and their authority for "harassment," or "wild goose chases," or "fishing expeditions."

In addition, a special idea of the way a lawyer should operate affects the division's treatment of its adversaries during the course of investigations. Again, division lawyers want to avoid giving the appearance of unreasonable harassment. For instance, they are well aware of the sometimes shady motives for which defense counsel request extensions of time in preparing their cases. But the staff says that it tends to grant these requests: The division lawyers feel a certain sympathy for the professional problems of their opposite members, and they do not consider it respectable to use constant demands and difficult time constraints as techniques for gaining advantage in a case. Private defense counsel, to be sure, do not agree about the generosity of the professional consideration the division offers them, but staff members do express the view that certain things cannot be done because they violate the civilities of good professional practice.

A final effect of this professionalism on the prosecutors' decisions can be seen in the ultimate judgment on possible cases for prosecution. It may be remembered that one young staff lawyer protested that the division's standards for judging a possible case were overly rigorous. He complained, "We're prosecutors. We should move on probable cause." In fact the front office does apply tests that in some ways are more stringent than that of "probable cause." Certainly one can point to the defects in the cases that the division does bring, but it remains true that merely bringing cases is not enough for the division's supervisory personnel. As we have seen, the chief reason for this caution is not mainly a fear for the division's fate with Congress or the Office of Management and Budget or the president but rather a wish, as one supervisor put it, that the division be seen as "the cream," and that it be looked upon with respect by its professional colleagues. Whether or not the division succeeds in its aim, the aim exists and has effect. One can well imagine a prosecutorial organization whose adversary impulse was less affected by this kind of concern for how adversaries would judge it; the division is not such an organization.

From looking at these sets of relationships—with business, with the rest of government, with the private bar—one might be tempted to say that the division "buys" its relative independence from regulated businessmen and other parts of the government at the price of tempering its prosecutorial impulse out of concern that its cases be deemed professionally worthy. But if a purchase is indeed involved one should not exaggerate the price that is paid. For one thing, the protection that the organization receives is substantial, and almost all participants in the antitrust policy area think it valuable. Just as important, the antitrust bar itself is by no means an opponent of antitrust enforcement in general; the bar cannot be called simply "antiprosecutorial." Some private antitrust lawyers are alumni of the division and retain many of the division's general opinions on antitrust matters. Moreover, any single government antitrust prosecution may benefit rather than harm the clients of a private defense attorney; aggressive efforts by the division may lead to the elimination of practices or structures harmful to some businessmen or make it easier to collect damages from offending parties. Further, the defense bar gets obvious benefits from its clients' being under direct attack by the division. And finally, the private antitrust bar expects prosecution from the division, expects an adversary relationship, certainly feels no shock or betrayal at such things, and therefore finds the adversary relationship itself no barrier to professional respect or even admiration. Thus while professional considerations do temper the division's prosecutions, there are reasons why this professional judgment neither consistently opposes prosecution nor attempts to measure the division's performance wholly in terms of the interests of its private clients. The profession's opinion can hardly be considered a major or monolithic constraint against prosecution.

Thus the division's own sense of an obligation to prosecute and other parties' awareness of this sense have an important effect on the organization's relations with its various attentive publics. But just as important, the prosecutorial ethos brings with it a characteristic conception of a satisfactory economy and of the agency's proper role in promoting such an economy. The lawyers enforce, of course, a generally procompetitive body of law, and their ideas of economic health are at the most general level consistent with this procompetitive stance. Almost all the division lawyers interviewed seemed confident that economic health and justice flow above all from maximum competition. And however this term is understood, however general it is, it does rule out certain habits of thought on the lawyers' part. The lawyers strongly oppose any attempts to balance the value of competition against that of other economic or social goods. They do not accept that major conflicts among these goals exist in the long run, and they accept neither general arguments in favor of more economic planning nor more specific arguments suggesting that some desired social goal will not be well served by maximum competition. They also resist suggestions that in specific cases the connection between competition and the conditions it is supposed to produce may be tenuous or nonexistent. In isolated cases, it is true, their recommendations may reflect a tacit acknowledgment that the goal of maximizing competition may in fact conflict with other desirable ends. But the massive presumption in favor of competition prevents other criteria from exercising a large or systematic influence on their decisions. When these competing standards do come to influence their decisions, the staff has considerable difficulty resolving the inconsistencies that arise; they may even criticize their superiors for making negative decisions on cases where noncompetition criteria had caused ambivalance in the staff itself.

But if there is this massive presumption within the division in favor of competition, it is not clear that its idea of competition is an economically coherent one: As recent critics have made clear, many division policies may easily be challenged on this score. First, on the question of the division as a rational economic decision maker, there is the simple and large problem of how resources are allocated within the division: The organization does tend to choose its cases from the materials immediately at hand rather than from a more systematic notion of where division action would make the largest contribution to competitive conditions in the economy.

Second, the urge to bring a "big" case affects the prevailing attitude toward the question of absolute size of firms under investigation. It would of course not be unreasonable to concentrate one's procompetitive efforts on large firms whose actions have large effects, but it appears that the presence of a large firm in an investigation will prompt not simply a search for the anticompetitive effects but a search that tends to construe even probably harmless things in an anticompetitive light. This cast of mind by no means allows the division to spend all its time attacking the nation's largest firms; we have seen how the organization's information structure and operating routines prevent such an allocation of resources. But we have also seen how the presence of bigness in a case at hand will convince many lawyers that they will find "something bad" about the situation if only they look long and hard enough.

In the same way, a prosecutor's definition of a "big" case, and the division's tendency to equate personal power with economic power, produce a special attitude toward small business. One should not overdraw the degree of the staff's solicitude. Almost all the division lawyers asked about the matter, for instance, wanted abolition of state "fair trade" laws even though these laws, which establish uniform retail prices for certain commodities, are claimed to enable some small businesses to survive in the presence of larger, more efficient competitors who would otherwise cut prices and drive their smaller rivals out of existence. Furthermore, the kind of information the division receives and the kind of antitrust violations that smaller firms seem more likely to commit combine to put much division time into the investigation and prosecution of smaller firms. Still, we have seen that many staff lawyers profess themselves more inclined to drop cases that involve firms of small absolute size or of small size relative to that of their competitors. Moreover, the staff speaks of hesitating even in actions against larger firms when they can see that their actions may have major adverse consequences for smaller ones.

Finally, the staff lawyers feel a strong obligation to prosecute certain kinds of cases not because they are of major economic significance, but because the practices involved are clearly illegal, or the cases can clearly be won or settled favorably, or because they involve a type of personal coercion that is particularly offensive. A boycott that has no significant effect on the overall competitive situation in a given area, a tie-in that may actually increase competition in one of the commodities involved, a case of reciprocity that establishes a form of competition in an area characterized by inflexible and uniform prices—such practices, along with many conduct violations that are simply very small—are likely to be at least proposed for attack by the division staff. As the lawyer who had pursued one economically insignificant case of exclusion remembered, "Sure it was small. But it was nasty." And the prevailing notion of what "nastiness" consists of is not wholly formed by economic reasoning.

Because all of these attitudes in the division are not fully consistent, because they can easily come into conflict, the organization's resistance to a single well-articulated set of criteria for prosecution or a single comprehensive plan of action is a useful one. A division lawyer interested in preserving his prosecutorial range and discretion would indeed resist formulations that might totally remove certain types of prosecutions from his reach, and in fact the division's present methods of operation serve to avoid such a constriction of opportunity.

Finally, the ambiguities in the law's interpretation and the prosecutorial response to these ambiguities affect not only division relationships with outside actors and attitudes toward economic principle but also the staff's stance toward the organization's hierarchy and toward changes that the organization's executive may attempt to institute. The organization has, for a group of professionals, a fairly tolerant attitude toward its executive hierarchy and a considerable capacity to accept changes that the executive makes. The conflict that most often takes place between the staff and the front office is the conflict between the desire to bring every case possible and the conflicting desires to protect the agency's reputation for legal competence and its win-lose record. Expressions of this conflict are numerous; almost every staff lawyer interviewed professed some degree of contempt for or irritation at what he considered the timorousness of the front office. But there are factors that limit the intensity of the conflict. Battle lines are not impermeable: The front office is not without its own desire to bring cases, and the staff itself is aware of the uses of a formidable reputation. Rejecting a case on what the staff would consider "technical" grounds does not violate its sense of integrity; arguments from lawyers' considerations are arguments staff lawyers respect.

When the terms of this ongoing debate have changed—when corruption at higher levels is suspected, or when the hierarchy has suggested that the staff misunderstands the very criteria that are to be brought into the balance when decisions are made—this tolerance disappears. Such a disappearance seems never to have brought about an open, major staff rebellion, but the quiet seems connected to the often-made staff observation that the preferences of any single assistant attorney general are a distinctly temporary phenomenon in the division's life.

In the same way, the organization displays a considerable tolerance toward most of the formal organizational changes it undergoes. Changes that do not directly threaten the criteria of prosecution have not been strongly resisted, even though they have sometimes absorbed significant parts of the organization's resources. And, finally, the staff is receptive to new arguments for and areas of prosecution that an executive may propose, even when his directives entail a significant reallocation of resources. It is when the lawyers' eclectic standards of choice are seen as threatened—when they are told to rely more exclusively than they see fit on one standard alone—that they will resist innovation. Here, too, the organization's behavior is powerfully affected by a desire to prosecute and to take full advantage of the opportunities for prosecution that ambiguities in the law provide.

Organization and Intention

A student of any sector of public policy and its administration
ought to feel responsible for evaluating both by measuring their
effects against the desired state that the policy was intended to
achieve and by comparing them to alternative means of achieving
that state of affairs. In the case of antitrust policy, however, such
evaluation is especially difficult, first because the "desired state"
that the laws intended is itself a subject of dispute. One body of
opinion sees in the current state of the law a fairly accurate though
pale reflection of our original policy intentions. This opinion sees
our chief legislative need as that of extending the law and its sanctions, and identifies underenforcement as the major problem of
antitrust administration.[1] Another opinion, relying on another
idea of the law's intent, holds that the original purpose of our antitrust policy has been more radically corrupted—that the law has
been applied not to the problems it was meant to meet but to
problems that do not exist. This second opinion holds that the
chief need in the field, though not the only need, is for doctrinal
correction.[2]

The first view of things, the view that sees the major existing
problem of antitrust enforcement not as a problem of intellect but
as one of political will, directs us to evaluate the Antitrust Division
by asking how well the organization has kept or can keep itself free
from the external corruptions of venality, clientalism, and political
interest. And if one uses these standards, one can make at least
some preliminary comparisons between the administrative form
the division embodies and the major alternative form of organization that was adopted during the same years to regulate business—that of the independent commission with broad rule-
making and administrative powers.

Now there are, of course, those who think that the question of
regulatory administration is a trivial one—that the problem of the
independent commissions lies not in any independent flaws of organization but rather in the very laws to be administered, in the
idea of supplanting the rules of competition. Of course, it is said,
such an idea will harm the welfare of producers and consumers
alike. But there are also those who contend that even insofar as

intervention in the market is necessary, commission regulation has failed—that there are organizational flaws, as distinct from the notion of regulation itself, that prevent the commissions from performing effectively and responsibly. The commissions are accused of having been co-opted by the industries under their jurisdiction and diverted from their proper allegiance to the interest of the public as a whole; they are accused of making bad decisions because of the intrusions of partisan politics; and they are accused of simple inattention to their primary goals, an inattention so pronounced that the regulators exist in American economic life only as a symbolic presence.

One response to these perceived flaws of the commission form has been an effort to curtail their traditionally broad discretion. It has been suggested—and by now action on the suggestion has more than begun—that congressional mandates should narrow the range of the laws that such agencies are empowered to enforce and put sharper limits on the criteria they may take into account when making decisions. It has further been suggested that agency discretion should also be limited by enabling courts to intervene more energetically and to pass judgment on the substantive merits as well as the procedural propriety of the regulatory decisions.

In judging this argument, we might remember that certain of the organizational arrangements that are now being advocated as means to regulatory reform are already to be found in the Justice Department's enforcement of the federal antitrust policy. The Antitrust Division occupies this "favored" position as a regulator for several reasons, of course, and some of them are unique to antitrust. The consensual nature of its goals and procedures gives it significant freedom from partisan interventions, more freedom in principle than many other regulators enjoy; and its dealings with many economic sectors whose interests are often in sharp conflict somewhat reduces the risk of co-optation over that faced by regulators of a more unified set of interests. But more important, the division has the characteristics specifically sought by today's regulatory reformers: The organization operates under a relatively specific mandate, and it must most definitely have recourse to the courts on a routine basis for its authority. These circumstances have indeed produced a characteristic pattern of behavior, one that is predominantly prosecutorial and professional rather than party-political or clientalist; the pattern is one that the current reformers would recognize and one that does not measure up so badly according to their standards.

The pattern in some respects seems capable of sustaining, over time, a faithfulness to legislative intentions. Most important, with isolated exceptions the Antitrust Division cannot be said to have been simply co-opted by business or industry in any intelligible sense of the term. The division rarely acts or refrains from acting out of a concern for the interests of prospective defendants as the defendants themselves understand these interests; it seeks to expand its domain rather than to restrict it; it acts in a way that minimizes its predictability; and it displays, in the main, not a systematic sympathy toward defendants' explanations and motives but mistrust.[3]

In the same way, it can reasonably be argued that the division has, more than the commissions to which its form is an alternative, escaped massive corruption by other interested parties. The division has by no means been free from attempts at such influence or scandals arising from these attempts. But the procedures and incentive structures that characterize its prosecutorial mode of behavior make it relatively difficult for such attempts to succeed.

Even when one examines the division's relations with the private antitrust bar, one sees that the organization has preserved a good deal of independence. Most important, the division does not behave so as to make itself predictable to the defense. It refuses to define its mission simply as one of establishing a clear and stable body of antitrust law; on the contrary, it seizes upon a significant number of opportunities to try to extend the reach of the law to cover actions and situations not clearly illegal under standing interpretations. In other words, one of the division's major tasks, as the organization's own staff sees it, is to create a permanently unstable relationship between itself and its professional public. Concern for the "quality" of cases may temper this impulse but cannot be said to prevent its expression, and this desire to extend the law serves to minimize the extent to which the division acts out of deference to received opinion in the antitrust bar as a whole. It is not surprising that despite the division's expressed attention to the legal profession, defense attorneys interviewed—especially those who had not served in the division—did not purport to find the division overwhelmingly reasonable in its choice of cases or polite and accommodating in its general behavior.

So according to one notion of what the antitrust law was intended for, the division's circumstances do give it a significant advantage in fulfilling some of the most important "contextual goals"[4] that we want our regulators to serve. But what if one employs the alternative notion? There remain, in other words, the questions of whether the present division makes anything like a measurably effective defense of some coherent notion of economic or business competition, and of whether its organization can be said to have anything to do with its performance in this regard.

Now in one sense—in the sense of actually knowing with some certainty what impact is made on the economy and on business practices by the antitrust work of the division and the courts—answering such questions is impossible: One can make determinations in some areas,[5] but there are certain remaining questions —about the prevalence of some kinds of conduct violations, especially criminal ones, or about the division's general deterrent effect—that stand in the way of any statement that is both general and determinate. Still, there is a broad consensus that there are some patently anticompetitive features of the economy that antitrust policy has so far proved unable to reach—most generally, as Richard Posner argues, forms of collusive pricing that do not generate detectable acts of communication among colluding sellers.[6] And there is a more controversial but substantial body of opinion arguing that at the same time the division attacks some practices that help competition rather than hinder it.[7]

One must judge that the division's behavior contributes to these failings in part because of its organizational virtues. More serious than the deviations from the prosecutorial ethic that professionalism may cause are problems that may arise in the division from the very prevalance and power of prosecutorial professionalism. For one thing, the division's commitment to prosecution does impose on the organization certain important limitations. It limits the kind of information the division gathers about the state of competition in the economy by favoring the gathering of that information that seems directly relevant to immediate prosecution. It limits the division's interpretation and use of the information it does have by imposing certain requirements of advocacy. The division's choice of strategy is associated with other features as well: The organization may mount large antitrust campaigns, but it cannot be said to concentrate its resources systematically on what seem to be the most economically significant matters, in part because of the attractiveness—at least to professional prosecutors—of cases that are easily prosecuted. It resists the choice of a single, coherent enforcement strategy and to some extent resists clarifications of law that might lend the field greater simplicity and stability at the risk of narrowing the field of possible action. And it has pursued the cases at hand, and pursued the general idea of extending the reach of the law, without consistent regard for a coherent notion of economic competition and of the division's role in promoting it.

But to say this is not simply to make the familiar judgment that yet another government organization has, in the most unsurprising way, narrowed its mandate to less than what a desirable policy would require. It is true that the organization has chosen, in the path of prosecution, a path that is different from the "amphibious" behavior that Hamilton and Till wished for it. But before one calls this a corruption, one might remember two things: first, that it is no accident that antitrust administrators should have been able to find in their legislative mandate the sanction for more than one notion of antitrust goals; and second, that the path of prosecution was as much a part of their mandate as was the substance of the law itself. It is a path that provides, as we have seen, considerable protection from some of the abuses that concern us at the moment, but it is a route that places limits on the possibilities for reasonable policy-making, limits that are just as definite as those limitations we see in the commission form. In other words, the present form of our antitrust administration—along with the consequences it brings—is perhaps not so much a distortion of original policy intention as a realization of the ambiguities in that intention.

The consequences of this ambiguity—its costs and its benefits —are ones that we may well decide are worth having in the case of antitrust. But in the past decade, this adversarial form has come to influence more and more of the substance and procedure of our economic regulation. Looking back over our many years of experience with that form, perhaps it is not too much to say that it has distinct advantages in protecting a set of values that might otherwise have been seriously eroded in our society and distinct disadvantages for producing an enforcement style notable for its lack of self-criticism and nonpartisan self-restraint. As policy makers are asked to extend such arrangements to influence more and more areas of economic life, they might well ask whether the antitrust prosecutor's particular mix of qualities are the ones we want to see in all the new regulatory enterprises that we have recently created and are likely to continue to create.

Notes

Chapter 1

1

This view was suggested in Samuel P. Huntington's seminal article, "The Marasmus of the ICC: The Commission, the Railroads and the Public Interest," *Yale Law Journal*, 61:4 (April 1952), 467–509. It was generalized by Marver Bernstein in *Regulating Business by Independent Commission* (Princeton: Princeton University Press, 1955). And it now informs much popular discussion of regulation. See the following reports prepared under the aegis of consumer advocate Ralph Nader: Edward F. Cox, *The Nader Report on the Federal Trade Commission* (New York: Baron, 1969); Robert C. Fellmeth, *The Interstate Commerce Omission: The Public Interest and the ICC* (New York: Grossman, 1970); James S. Turner, *The Chemical Feast* (New York: Grossman, 1970).

2

See, for example, Bernard Schwartz, *The Professor and the Commissions* (New York: Knopf, 1959).

3

See, for example, Kenneth C. Davis, "Due Processitis in the AEC," *American Bar Association Journal*, 47:8 (August 1961), 782–785; Henry J. Friendly, *The Federal Administrative Agencies* (Cambridge, Mass.: Harvard University Press, 1962); Louis L. Jaffe, "The Effective Limits of the Administrative Process: A Re-evaluation," *Harvard Law Review* 67:7 (May 1954), 1105–1135.

4

See, for example, J. Murray Edelman, *The Symbolic Uses of Politics* (Urbana, Ill.: University of Illinois Press, 1964); Gabriel Kolko, *Railroads and Regulation, 1877–1916* (Princeton: Princeton University Press, 1965); and *The Triumph of Conservatism* (Glencoe, Ill.: The Free Press of Glencoe, 1963).

5

See Theodore Lowi, *The End of Liberalism* (New York: Norton, 1969), chap. 10.

6

See Paul H. Weaver, "Unlocking the Gilded Cage of Regulation," *Fortune* 94:2 (February 1977), 178–188.

7

See Simon Lazarus, *The Genteel Populists* (New York: Holt, Rinehart & Winston, 1974), chap. 10.

8

15 U.S.C. secs. 1–7 (Supp. I 1975).

9

15 U.S.C. secs. 12–27, 44; 29 U.S.C. 52–53.

10

In 1974, the attorney general's office announced that it would no longer review the division's recommendations on a routine basis.

11

The figure is from Richard A. Posner, *Antitrust Law: An Economic Perspective* (Chicago: University of Chicago Press, 1976), p. 25.

12

Ibid., passim.

13

See, for example, Daniel P. Moynihan, *Maximum Feasible Misunderstanding* (New York: Free Press, 1969), chaps. 4, 5.

Chapter 2

1

This account is drawn largely from Hans P. Thorelli, *The Federal Antitrust Policy* (Baltimore: Johns Hopkins University Press, 1954) and William Letwin, *Law and Economic Policy in America* (Edinburgh: Edinburgh University Press, 1966).

2

Thorelli, *Federal Antitrust Policy,* p. 144.

3

Ibid.

4

Ibid., p. 143.

5

Ibid.

6

Ibid., p. 138.

7

Letwin, *Law and Economic Policy,* p. 55.

8

Thorelli, *Federal Antitrust Policy,* p. 142.

9

Thorelli supports this view.

10

Henry George, *Progress and Poverty* (New York: Modern Library, 1938).

11
Edward Bellamy, *Looking Backward, 2000–1887* (Cambridge, Mass.: Harvard University Press, 1967).

12
See, for example, Henry D. Lloyd, "The Story of a Great Monopoly," *Atlantic Monthly* 47 (March 1881), 317–334; "Making Bread Dear," *North American Review* 137 (August 1883), 118–136; "Lords of Industry," *North American Review* 138 (June 1884), 535–553.

13
Thorelli, *Federal Antitrust Policy*, p. 109.

14
Ibid., p. 110.

15
Letwin, *Law and Economic Policy*, p. 71.

16
Thorelli, *Federal Antitrust Policy*, p. 120.

17
Letwin, *Law and Economic Policy*, p. 71.

18
Ibid., p. 73; Thorelli, *Federal Antitrust Policy*, p. 123.

19
Letwin, *Law and Economic Policy*, p. 76.

20
Thorelli, *Federal Antitrust Policy*, p. 166.

21
Ibid. p. 200.

22
Ibid.

23
Ibid., pp. 190, 198.

24
Ibid., p. 190.

25
Ibid., p. 180.

26
Ibid., pp. 180–181.

27
Robert Bork, "Legislative Intent and the Policy of the Sherman Act," *Journal of Law and Economics* 9 (October 1966), 7–48.

28

In interpreting Sherman as a modern-day economist, there also remains the problem of the appropriateness of such an interpretation to his legislative career as a whole—to, for instance, his non–free market prescriptions for the treatment of the tariff issue. See John Sherman, *Recollections of 40 Years in the House, Senate, and Cabinet: An Autobiography* (Chicago: The Werner Company, 1895), 2:1008. Indeed, one of the attacks made on Sherman during the course of the Sherman Act debates pointed out that large trusts were supported in no small part by the relatively restrictive tariff position that Sherman favored. Ibid., p. 1010, and Theodore Elijah Burton, *John Sherman* (Boston: Houghton Mifflin, 1906), p. 360.

29

Sherman made the political analogy in even stronger, more direct terms. Burton, *John Sherman*, p. 359, records him as saying, "If the concentered powers of this combination are intrusted to a single man, it is a kingly prerogative inconsistent with our form of government, and should be subject to the strong resistance of the state and national authorities. If anything is wrong, this is."

30

Bork, "Legislative Intent."

31

Thorelli, *Federal Antitrust Policy*, p. 61.

32

Ibid., p. 181.

33

The following account is drawn from Letwin, *Law and Economic Policy*, chap. 2.

34

Thorelli, *Federal Antitrust Policy*, p. 61.

35

Letwin, *Law and Economic Policy*, p. 85.

36

Thorelli, *Federal Antitrust Policy*, p. 184.

37

Neither the passage of the Clayton Act in 1914 nor its strengthening by amendment in 1950 seems to have been intended to contradict this approach. See Henry R. Seager and Charles A. Gulick, *Trust and Corporation Problems* (New York: Harper, 1929) and David D. Martin, *Mergers and the Clayton Act* (Berkeley: University of California Press, 1950).

38
Richard A. Posner, *Antitrust Law: An Economic Perspective* (Chicago: University of Chicago Press, 1976), p. 25.

39
Letwin, *Law and Economic Policy,* chap. 5.

40
Ibid., p. 183.

41
Posner, *Antitrust Law.*

42
Ibid.

43
Edward P. Hodges, "Complaints of Antitrust Violations and Their Investigation: The Work of the Complaints Section of the Antitrust Division," *Law and Contemporary Problems* 7:1 (Winter 1940), 90–95.

44
Posner, *Antitrust Law.*

45
The division's general correspondence is in the U.S. National Archives' File 60-0-10.

46
Posner, *Antitrust Law*. For an interesting comparison with the fate of a similar agency during this period, see G. Cullom Davis, "The Transformation of the FTC, 1914–1929," *Mississippi Historical Review* 49:3 (December 1962), 437–455.

47
See Ellis Hawley, *The New Deal and the Problem of Monopoly* (Princeton: Princeton University Press, 1966) and Francis Biddle, *In Brief Authority* (New York: Doubleday, 1962).

48
Hodges, "Complaints of Antitrust Violations."

49
During the years 1933 through 1937, five press releases were issued concerning the Justice Department's antitrust activities. Arnold raised the level to over fifty per year.

50
Posner, *Antitrust Law.*

51
Corwin D. Edwards, "Thurman Arnold and the Antitrust Laws," *Political Science Quarterly* 58:3 (September 1943), 338–355.

52
The speeches are reproduced in *Law and Contemporary Problems* 7:1
(Winter 1940).

53
Hodges, "Complaints of Antitrust Violations"; Charles L. Terrel, "Pro-
cesses in the Investigation of Complaints," *Law and Contemporary
Problems* 7:1 (Winter 1940), 99–103.

54
Thurman Arnold, "Antitrust Law Enforcement, Present and Future,"
Law and Contemporary Problems 7:1 (Winter 1940).

55
Hodges, "Complaints of Antitrust Violations," p. 90.

56
Ibid., p. 95.

57
Edwards, "Thurman Arnold."

58
Hodges, "Complaints of Antitrust Violations."

59
Ibid.

60
Terrel, "Processes," p. 99.

61
Walton Hamilton and Irene Till, *Antitrust in Action,* Monograph No. 16
of the U.S. Temporary National Economic Commission, Investigation
of Concentration of Economic Power (Washington, D.C.: U.S. Government Printing Office, 1940), pp. 27–30.

62
Ibid., pp. 33–35.

Chapter 3

1
It must be noted, though, that at the time these interviews were conducted, economists constituted less than 10 percent of the division's
professional personnel. In spite of efforts to increase the use of economics in the division, they still constitute less than 10 percent.

2
Since the interview period, the proportion of older lawyers has dropped because of retirements.

3

The department estimated in 1976 that about half the division's new lawyers are now hired through the program.

4

From 1950 through 1954, the division brought three cases involving acquisition short of monopoly. By the period 1955 through 1959, the number had risen to twenty-six. These are among the figures gathered and analyzed by Richard A. Posner in "A Statistical Study of Antitrust Enforcement," *The Journal of Law and Economics* 13:2 (October 1970), 365–419.

5

John Herling, in *The Great Price Conspiracy* (Washington: Luce, 1962).

6

Ibid.

7

The division's statistics on the destinations of departing attorneys are not complete. But, in 1949, none were recorded as having left for private law firms or industry; in 1959, the figure was four out of seventeen, and by 1964, it had reached the level of sixteen out of twenty-one.

8

The ratio of applications to acceptances is high. In 1976, the honors program accepted 214 of its 2219 applicants. But the last available compilation of applicant characteristics, from 1973, indicates that two of the department's 108 successful honors program applicants had placed first in their law school classes, eight more within the top five.

Chapter 4

1

The division keeps, as far as I could discover, no totally inclusive listing—comprehending not only specific complaints but reports and leads from other sources—of items that are given at least some examination.

2

Division personnel say that the relevant information in such reports has usually come to the division's attention from other sources as well.

3

The division lawyers, to judge by these interviews, hold generally the same stance toward the idea of organizational hierarchy as is described by Peter M. Blau and Richard W. Scott in their discussion of professionalism. See their *Formal Organization* (San Francisco: Chandler, 1962), pp. 60–74, 244–247. But the presence of professionalism in the division does not produce the same intense disaffection and distance from the organization Blau and Scott find; as we shall see, the division reveals a substantial though not by any means perfect coincidence between the authority of office and the authority of expertise. And because areas of coincidence exist, one must be interested not simply in possible conflicts between hierarchy and professionalism in the division but in the substance of the professional values that have powerful effects at all levels of the hierarchy.

4
This degree and kind of reinforcement are by no means universal for government legal organizations. See James Eisenstein, "Counsel for the U.S.: An Empirical Analysis of the Office of U.S. Attorney" (Ph.D. dissertation, Yale University, 1968) and John T. Eliff, "The U.S. Department of Justice, 1937–1962" (Ph.D. dissertation, Harvard University, 1968).

5
Systematic figures on costs per case were unavailable from the division.

6
This account is drawn from A. D. Neale, *The Antitrust Laws of the U.S.A.* (Cambridge: Cambridge University Press, 1970).

7
On occasion, the division has resisted bringing certain kinds of cases in behalf of parties with the interest and resources to proceed privately. This resistance does not seem to occur with any great frequency.

8
The following account of structural violations is also drawn from Neale, *Antitrust Laws*.

9
A few staff lawyers do report higher proportions of positive recommendations.

10
For instance, various kinds of exemptions exist for regulated industries, for export associations, for agricultural cooperatives, for concerted action in dealing with governmental bodies, for labor unions, for patented products. See Neal, *Antitrust Laws,* for an introduction.

11
Associated Press v. *United States* (S.C. 1945), in which it was decided that the Associated Press, by denying its near-unique services to its members' competitors, was engaging in illegal restraint of trade.

Chapter 6

1

The decision relied on for this opinion was that of the Supreme Court in the case of *Federal Trade Commission* v. *Consolidated Foods* (1965).

2

See, for example, *U.S.* v. *U.S. Steel* (D. Pa. 1969) or *U.S.* v. *Kennecott Copper* (S.D.N.Y. 1971).

3

U.S.C. 1828(c).

4

See, for example, the Supreme Court's opinion in the case of *U.S.* v. *Procter and Gamble* (1967).

5

See, for example, *U.S.* v. *The First National Bank of Jackson and the Bank of Greenwood* (S.D. Miss. 1968).

6

See, for example, the discussions in Joe S. Bain, *Barriers to New Competition* (Cambridge, Mass.: Harvard University Press, 1956) and Frederic Scherer, *Industrial Market Structure and Economic Performance* (Chicago: Rand McNally, 1970).

7

For reflections by a participant on the division's experience with the "potential competition" argument in banking, see Donald I. Baker, "Potential Competition in Banking: After Greeley, What?" *The Banking Law Journal* 90:5 (May 1973), 362–380.

8

See the following statements: U.S., Congress, House, Staff of the Antitrust Subcommittee, Committee on the Judiciary, *The Celler-Kefauver Act: Sixteen Years of Enforcement* (committee print), 90th Cong., 1st sess., 1967, pp. 32–34; *Hearings on the Status and Future of Small Business before the Senate Select Committee on Small Business,* 90th Cong., 1st sess., 1967, Part 2, pp. 479–495; Willard F. Mueller, "The Rising Economic Concentration in America: Reciprocity, Conglomeration and the New American 'Zaibatsu' System," *Antitrust Law and Economics Review* 4:3 (Spring 1971), 15–50 and 4:4 (Summer 1971), 91–105.

9

See, for example, *U.S.* v. *International Telephone and Telegraph* (D. Conn. 1969).

10

See Donald F. Turner, "The Scope of Antitrust and Other Economic Regulatory Policies," *Harvard Law Review* 82:6 (April 1969), 1207–1244.

11

The guidelines are reproduced in A. D. Neale, *The Antitrust Laws of the U.S.A.* (Cambridge: Cambridge University Press, 1970), pp. 494–505.

12

It may also be remembered that the patents task force was established during this period.

13

For instance, the section soon became heavily involved in interventions by the division before the Federal Communications Commission and the Securities and Exchange Commission, as well as in litigation in the securities area—for example, *U.S.* v. *Chicago Board of Trade* (N.D. Ill. 1971), *Thill* v. *New York Stock Exchange* (E.D. Wisc. 1972).

Chapter 7

1

For one set of examples of the method as it was known at the time, see David Novick, ed., *Program Budgeting* (Cambridge, Mass.: Harvard University Press, 1965).

2

See Elizabeth Drew, "HEW Grapples with PPBS," *The Public Interest* 8 (Summer 1967), 9–29; Thomas C. Schelling, "PPBS and Foreign Affairs," *The Public Interest* 11 (Spring 1968), 26–36; and, more generally, Aaron Wildavsky, *Budgeting* (Boston: Little, Brown, 1975), chaps. 13–18.

3

At this writing, the chairman is Congressman John Slack.

4

U.S., Congress, House, Committee on Appropriations: Departments of State, Justice, Commerce, and the Judiciary, and Related Agency Appropriations, *Hearings*, 84th Cong., 1st sess. to 94th Cong., 1st sess., 1955–1975.

5

U.S., Congress, House, Committee on Appropriations: Departments of State, Justice, Commerce, and the Judiciary, and Related Agency Appropriations, *Hearings*, 91st Cong., 1st sess., 1969, pp. 784–785.

6

U.S., Congress, House, Committee on Appropriations: Departments of State, Justice, Commerce, and the Judiciary, and Related Agency Appropriations, *Hearings*, 91st Cong., 2nd sess., 1970, p. 561.

7

Ibid., p. 555.

8
U.S., Congress, House, Committee on Appropriations: Departments of State, Justice, Commerce, and the Judiciary, and Related Agency Appropriations, *Hearings*, 92nd Cong., 1st sess., 1971, p. 1222.

9
U.S., Congress, House, Committee on Appropriations: Departments of State, Justice, Commerce, and the Judiciary, and Related Agency Appropriations, *Hearings*, 93rd Cong., 1st sess., 1973, pp. 1033–1034.

10
This account is in its important respects consistent with the more general description by Aaron Wildavsky in *The Politics of the Budgetary Process* (Boston: Little, Brown, 1964), pp. 64–111.

11
U.S., Congress, Senate, Committee on the Judiciary, *Drug Industry Antitrust Act: Hearings before the Senate Subcommittee on Antitrust and Monopoly*, 87th Cong., 1st sess., 1961, pp. 2610–2619.

12
U.S., Congress, Senate, Committee on the Judiciary, *Possible Anticompetitive Effects of the Sale of Network Television Advertising: Hearings before the Senate Subcommittee on Antitrust and Monopoly*, 89th Cong., 1st sess., 1966, pp. 651-657.

13
U.S., Congress, Senate, Committee on the Judiciary, *Economic Concentration: Hearings before the Senate Subcommittee on Antitrust and Monopoly*, 89th Cong., 1st sess., 1965, pp. 809–830.

14
"Possible Anticompetitive Effects," p. 656.

15
U.S., Congress, Senate, Committee on the Judiciary, *International Aspects of Antitrust: Hearings before the Senate Subcommittee on Antitrust and Monopoly*, 89th Cong., 1st sess., 1965, pp. 496-511.

16
U.S., Congress, Senate, Committee on the Judiciary, *A Study of the Antitrust Laws: Hearings before the Senate Subcommittee on Antitrust and Monopoly*, 81st Cong., 1st sess., 1955, pp. 4–33.

17
Ibid., pp. 281–366. This congressional treatment of the way the agency makes its decisions in specific cases contrasts sharply with the treatment accorded some other economy-regulating agencies. See, for example, the discussion of the National Labor Relations Board in Seymour Scher's "Congressional Committee Members as Independent

Agency Overseers: A Case Study," *American Political Science Review*
54:4 (December 1960), 911–920.

18
Most important, 1974 amendments significantly increased maximum
penalties under the Sherman Act.

19
See Mark J. Green, ed., *The Closed Enterprise System* (Washington,
D.C.: Center for the Study of Responsive Law, 1971).

20
Ibid., pp. 73–74.

21
Ibid., pp. 83–84.

22
Ibid., p. 69.

23
Ibid.

24
See *The New York Times*, July 20, 1974, p. 13.

25
The ABA as a whole has 215,834 members out of the country's 425,039
lawyers.

Chapter 8

1
Mark J. Green, ed., *The Closed Enterprise System* (Washington, D.C.:
Center for the Study of Responsive Law, 1971).

2
Richard A. Posner, *Antitrust Law: An Economic Perspective* (Chicago:
University of Chicago Press, 1976).

3
Businessmen have even stronger opinions on the subject of the division. In 1970, *Fortune* magazine asked a panel of chief executives of
business firms, "Which federal agency have you found most difficult
to deal with?" The Antitrust Division received by far the largest number of votes as "most difficult" (24 percent of the panel gave it this
distinction). The Federal Trade Commission was next with 16 percent,
and no other government agency received more than 7 percent. As
one panelist remarked, "I feel the Antitrust Division is overzealous in
trying to enforce new laws rather than just enforcing the existing interpretation of the laws." Robert S. Diamond, "What Business Thinks:
The Fortune 500–Yankelovich Survey," *Fortune* (January 1970), 123–124.

4
The term is from James Q. Wilson, "The Bureaucracy Problem," *The Public Interest* 6 (Winter 1967), 3–9.

5
See, for example, George Stigler, "The Economic Effects of the Antitrust Laws," *Journal of Law and Economics* 9 (October 1966), 225–258.

6
Posner, *Antitrust Law,* chap. 4.

7
Ibid., chap. 8.

Index